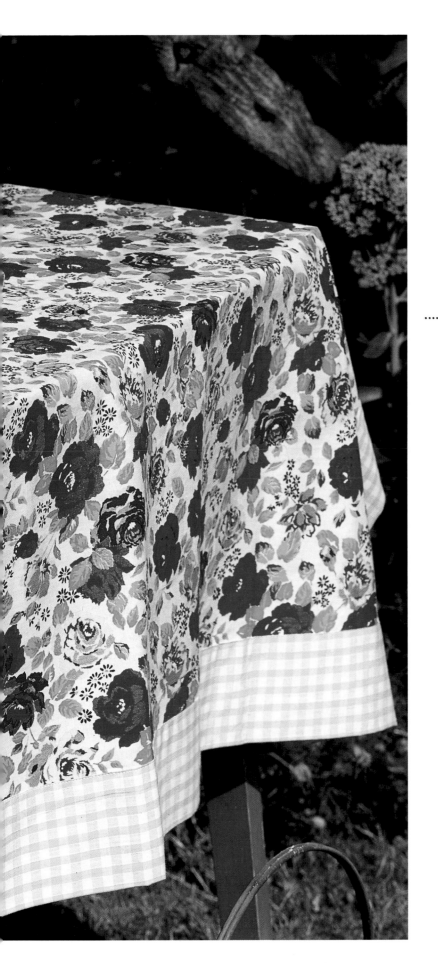

LEARN
TO
SEW

CHRIS JEFFERYS

NEW
HOLLAND

Reprinted in 2010
This paperback edition first published in 2008 by
New Holland Publishers (UK) Ltd
London · Cape Town · Sydney · Auckland

Garfield House, 86–88 Edgware Road
London W2 2EA
United Kingdom
www.newhollandpublishers.com

80 McKenzie Street
Cape Town 8001
South Africa

Unit 1, 66 Gibbes Street
Chatswood, NSW 2067
Australia

218 Lake Road
Northcote, Auckland
New Zealand

ISBN 978 1 84773 228 6

Senior Editors: Clare Sayer, Steffanie Brown
Production: Hazel Kirkman
Design: Frances de Rees
Photographer: Shona Wood
Illustrations: Carrie Hill
Editorial Direction: Rosemary Wilkinson

5 7 9 10 8 6

Reproduction by Pica Digital PTE Ltd, Singapore
Printed and bound by Times Offset (M) Sdn. Bhd., Malaysia

LEARN TO SEW

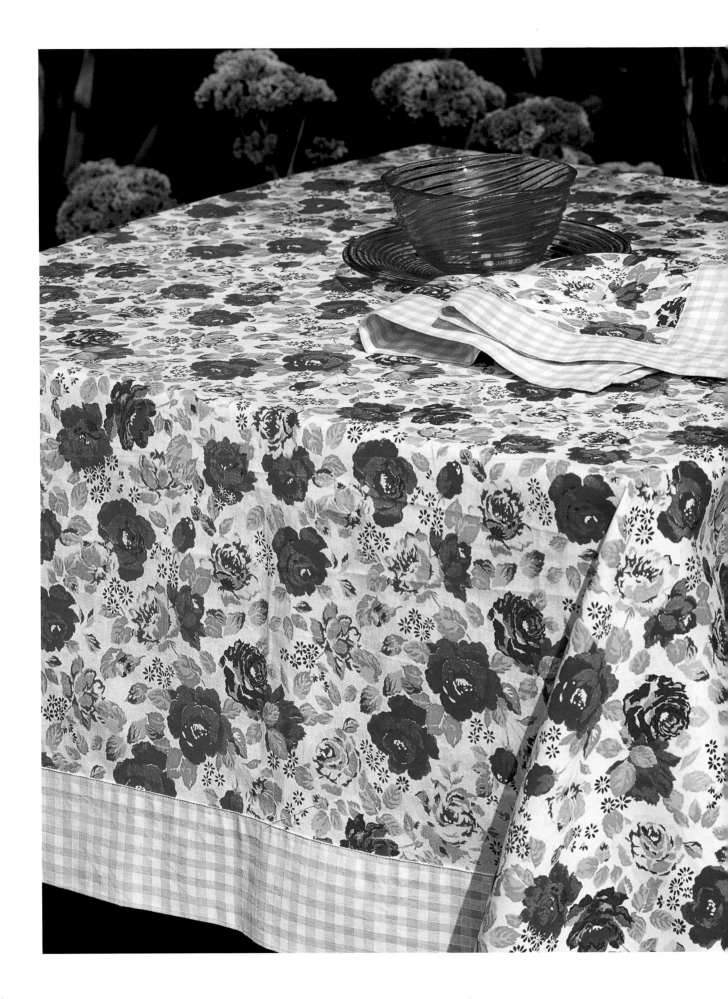

CONTENTS

INTRODUCTION

Sewing is the art of joining together and embellishing pieces of fabric to make items that can be both decorative and functional. Both a practical and creative hobby, sewing your own items can not only help you cut down expenses; it can also be very rewarding as a creative outlet in your life, letting you add your personal touch to create original items for your family and home.

This book will lead you step by step through all the basic techniques you need to know in order to sew beautiful, sturdy garments. Essential information about sewing is detailed at the start of the book, to introduce you to the various tools and materials used in the craft. This general information is followed by detailed instructions on basic techniques such as cutting, making seams and hems, binding, joining, mitring and stitching, as well as information on how to create "finishing touches" such as appliqués, to make your work look really exquisite. Each technique is then followed by a project that employs the skills that you have just learned. All of the projects in the book have been specially chosen to help you build your confidence and skills in each given technique, and also to teach you how to make stylish, beautiful garments and décor items in the simplest of ways.

Throughout the book you'll also find clever ideas for making alterations and repairs to your favourite old garments and household items. These sections will inspire you to take out a new lease on the life of a favourite dress or curtains, or to mend that hole in your pocket through which your coins keep falling! Once you have mastered the basics of this wonderfully creative craft, you can use your imagination to work with the colours and textures of your own chosen fabrics and trimmings and make your own inspired individual pieces.

Chris Jefferys

Basic Information

Choosing the right fabric and good basic equipment will make it easier to develop your sewing skills, and will help produce successful projects. While most sewing equipment is relatively inexpensive, a sewing machine is a somewhat pricey investment and should be considered carefully.

A GOOD BASIC SEWING KIT

While there are many sewing aids that you will undoubtedly find useful as your skills progress, the items described here form a good basic kit. As a general rule it is always worthwhile buying the best-quality items you can afford, especially when it comes to scissors and pins.

● A pack of assorted needles
● A box of dressmaker's pins
● Dressmaker's cutting out scissors or shears
● Small, sharp scissors for snipping threads and fabrics
● A ruler and a right-angle set square for drawing and measuring straight lines
● A tape measure for measuring lengths
● An erasable fabric marker pen, a sharp pencil or dressmaker's chalk
● A good quality steam iron (to be used between each stage of making up)
● An ironing board (keep it set up all the time to encourage good pressing habits)

SEWING MACHINES

There are many types of sewing machines on the market at a great range of prices, a fact that can be both bewildering and intimidating for a beginner. When thinking about which type of sewing machine to buy, the most important consideration is that of which types of stitches you will use most often for the sewing work you intend to do. That said, a good basic machine selection includes a straight stitch, a zigzag stitch, a three-step or tricot zigzag stitch, a blind hemming stitch and a buttonhole stitch.

Straight stitch

The straight stitch is the basic machine stitch used for stitching seams. The size of the stitches can be lengthened or shortened, but a medium-length stitch is the one used for most types of sewing. The straight stitch can be lengthened to the longest length on the machine to make a gathering stitch. Straight stitching is worked in reverse at the beginning and end of a seam to fasten off the thread ends and prevent unravelling.

Zigzag stitch

The zigzag stitch is worked over raw edges in order to make them neater, and to prevent the fabric from fraying. The stitch length can be adjusted lengthways to space the stitches further apart or closer together; it can also be adjusted widthways to make the stitch wider or narrower. A medium stitch in both length and width is usually best for making the edges of a garment look neater. The zigzag stitch can also be adjusted so that the stitches are close together. Stitches made in this way, which are commonly known as satin stitches, form the basic stitch for buttonholes, and are also commonly used to stitch appliqué.

Three-step zigzag or tricot stitch

A variation on the zigzag stitch, the three-step zigzag or tricot stitch has three small stitches along each leg of the zigzag. This stitch can be adjusted in the same ways as the zigzag stitch, and is similarly used to make fabric edges look neater. On some fabrics, especially fine ones, use of a regular zigzag stitch will roll the edge of the fabric over, forming an

unwanted ridge. Use of the three-step version avoids this result, giving a flatter finish. The three-step zigzag stitch is also handy for joining the ends of elasticised fabrics, and for stitching around the overlapped edges of a patch, such as on a sheet.

Blind hem stitch

This special hem stitch is worked on hems that are folded back on themselves. It stitches a few straight stitches along the hem fold,

then swings across in a single zigzag to catch the main fabric. This type of stitch can be an easier option to hand-stitching on long, straight hems, such as are necessary for curtains, but it is arguably too complicated to set up for short lengths.

Buttonhole stitch

Always try out the buttonhole stitch on any sewing machine you are contemplating purchasing. Many machines have automatic one-step buttonhole stitch-makers, which do not always make good buttonholes. While two-step or four-step buttonhole stitch-makers may seem complicated at first glance, they are actually quite easy to operate. A good buttonhole stitch-maker will have the stitches stitched forward, and those that are stitched backward will be the same distance apart. There will also be a clean channel along the centre through which to cut.

CHOOSING FABRICS

The choice of fabric is a very important part of a successful project. As well as looking at the colour and pattern of the fabric, always feel it as well, to see how it handles. Learn to distinguish between fabrics with body, which will give shape to the item, and stiff fabrics, which may be treated with a dressing that will wash out, leaving them limp and creased. On lightweight fabrics, hold up a length to check that it will gather and hang well, making sure it is a "fine" fabric as opposed to a flimsy one! Check to see what the fabric looks like when it is creased by screwing up a corner and then releasing it. If in doubt, look and feel a fabric that has been used in a ready-made item to see how it suits its purpose.

Cotton

One of the most versatile and popular fabrics, cotton is ideal for many of the projects shown in this book. A natural fabric made from the hairs that cover the seed pod of the cotton plant, it is available in light to medium weights.

Cotton fabrics handle well, do not fray easily

BELOW, anti-clockwise from left: steam iron, assorted needles and pins, dressmaker's shears, small scissors, tape measure, ruler, dressmaker's chalk, erasable fabric marker pen, right-angle set square, sewing machine.

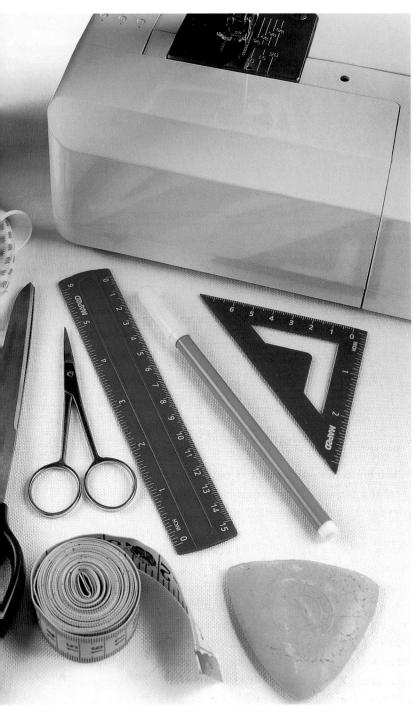

and respond well to pressing. There are many different types of cotton fabrics, as they vary according to their weave and finish. Some of the most popular cotton fabrics include gingham, chambray, poplin, denim, chintz, drill, ticking, cambric and calico. Lighter-weight cottons include lawn and voile, both of which can be used for lightweight curtains.

Silk

Another beautiful natural fabric, silk is made from the pupae of the silkworm. Its inherent properties enable it to absorb dyes easily. This ability, together with its natural sheen, produces a wonderful range of deep, strong colours that cannot be achieved in other fabrics. Silk will crease a little more easily than cotton, but it presses well. Silk fabrics are prone to fraying and can be slippery to handle, so a beginner who wants to use them is advised to start with a very simple project. Silk dupion is a lightweight silk with a reasonably firm handle. It has an uneven slub weave that is part of its charm. Silk organza is very lightweight and sheer.

Wool

Made from sheep's wool, woollen fabric can be woven in many ways, creating a range of fabrics varying from fine wool challis to thick, hairy tweed. Woollen fabrics are generally warm, resist fraying and handle well. These fabrics are used mainly for clothing.

Linen

Linen fabrics are made from the fibres of the flax plant, and are woven into light- to medium-weight fabrics. Most linens resist fraying and handle well, but are prone to creasing by virtue of the fabric's natural character. That said, the gorgeous sheen of linen is often thought to offset this drawback.

Man-made fabrics

Man-made fabrics are made from either chemicals or reformed cellulose, and include polyester, nylon and rayon. Some of these fabrics are slippery and crease easily, while others, like polyester, are very crease-resistant. Man-made fibres are often mixed with natural fibres to produce a fabric possessing the best qualities of both fabrics. For example, polyester cotton voile has all the advantages of cotton together with the crease resistance of polyester.

CHOOSING THREADS

Threads are used for both hand- and machine-stitching. There are various types of threads on the market; choose according to fabric, permanence and personal preference.

BELOW, clockwise from bottom right: grey and purple wools, white and blue linens, blue paisley and yellow polyester fabrics, blue checked cotton, green silk dupion, pink silk organza, yellow checked cotton, cotton flower print.

Tacking thread

Tacking thread is a loosely twisted cotton thread used only for temporary tacking, as it is not strong enough for permanent stitching. Some cheap tacking threads can deposit pinpricks of loose dye onto light fabrics, so be careful when using these threads.

Cotton thread

Cotton thread is a fine, mercerized thread that is used for hand- and machine stitching, usually on natural fabrics such as cotton, linen and woollen fabrics.

Polyester thread

This is a popular, multipurpose type of thread that can be used on all types of fabrics. It is strong and comes in a wide range of colours. It is used for both hand- and machine stitching.

Silk thread

Silk thread is a fine, yet strong thread that can be used for both hand- and machine stitching. It is used commonly on silk and wool fabrics, and for hand-stitched buttonholes on finer fabrics.

Bold thread

Sometimes called buttonhole twist, bold thread is a strong, thick thread that is used mainly for hand-stitching when extra strength is required. It is also used for hand-stitching buttonholes on heavier-weight garments.

CHOOSING NEEDLES AND PINS

Needles and pins will slip more easily through fabric if they are both fine and sharp. Choose a needle as fine as you can thread easily – a pack of assorted sewing needles is a good choice to start with. Thick needles or pins are difficult to push through fabric, and may leave unsightly holes on some fabrics.

Sewing machine needles

Most sewing machines come supplied with a packet of needles in various sizes, from 9 to 16 (the higher the number, the thicker the needle). A medium 11 or 14 works best for most fabrics, but the general rule is that the finer the fabric, the finer the required needle. If you break a needle while sewing, keep its flat side in the same position when replacing it so that the needle can catch the thread.

Pins

Pins are available with small metal heads or larger glass or pearl heads. The latter type can be easier to pick up and handle, but the choice is a personal preference. Extra-fine lace pins are available, but are really only needed for fine bridal and evening fabrics.

ABOVE, top row: packet of sewing machine needles; middle row, from left: polyester bold thread, cotton thread, polyester tacking thread, silk thread, polyester thread; bottom row, from left: pins with pearl heads, pins with small metal heads.

Getting Started

Before you start any sewing project, there are some essential techniques you will need to learn. This section takes you through the first stages, from pinning and tacking to basic seams.

CUTTING YOUR FABRIC

Careful cutting out is the first step to success in any sewing project, however simple. All you need is a long ruler, a right-angle set square, a marker pen and good dressmaking shears (bent-handled ones are easiest to use).

Fabric is made in long lengths with finished edges called selvedges along the two side edges. Most fabrics are woven from two sets of threads: the warp threads which run along the length of the fabric parallel to the selvedges and the weft threads which run across the fabric between the selvedges. The grain of the fabric follows the line of one of these sets of threads. Ensure your fabric pieces are cut out accurately along the grain of the fabric.

To establish the widthways grain, trim the edge along the line of a woven stripe or check, or pull out a thread across the width of the fabric and trim along the drawn line. On fabric where neither of these methods is suitable, the grain will need to be drawn at right angles to the selvedge, using a right-angle set square as a guide. Pieces are usually cut out with the warp threads running down the item and the weft threads running across, though at times this is reversed for special effect.

FINDING THE BIAS

The bias or crossway of the fabric runs diagonally across the fabric. To establish the bias, fold the fabric diagonally so the across grain edge is parallel to the lengthways grain and selvedges. The diagonal fold is now on the bias (**A**). To make bias or crossway strips, cut along this fold. You can then cut strips to the required width along the cut edge.

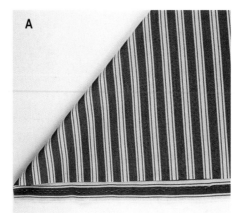

PINNING AND TACKING

Before stitching any two pieces of fabric, you will need to pin and tack them together. Tacking is temporary stitching used to hold the fabric prior to it being machine- or hand-stitched. Use ordinary thread or specialist tacking thread – it is a good idea to use a contrast colour so you can remove the tacking stitches easily.

1. Place the edges to be joined together with right sides facing and the raw edges level. Pin the two layers together with the pins at right angles to the edge, or with pins along the seamline 1.5 cm ($\frac{5}{8}$ in) in from the edge. Space the pins about 5 cm (2 in) apart, or further on firm fabrics.

2. Begin and finish tacking with one or two backstitches worked one on top of the other. Tack by stitching in and out through the layers of fabric, making stitches 1–1.5 cm ($\frac{3}{8}$–$\frac{5}{8}$ in) long and in a line 1.5 cm ($\frac{5}{8}$ in) from the raw edges (**B**). Work the tacking over the crossways pins and then remove the pins.

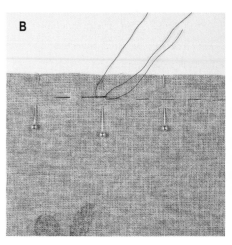

3. On the lengthways pinning, remove the pins as they are reached. Remove the tacking after the seam is stitched.

JOINING FABRICS

Most sewing projects involve stitching together two or more fabric pieces with seams, to make a larger piece of fabric or to make an item. This can either be done by machine or by hand. Machine-stitching is obviously much quicker and generally stronger, although sometimes, particularly on small areas, it is easier to stitch by hand.

Running stitch

This simple handstitch is useful on small areas, but is not very strong. Working from right to left, stitch along the seamline, taking the needle down through the two layers then back up again. Keep the stitches small and gather a few onto the needle before pulling the needle through (**C**). The smaller the stitches, the neater and stronger the seam.

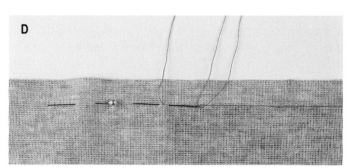

Backstitch

This is the strongest of the handstitches. Working along the seamline, take the needle down through the fabric and bring it back up about 3 mm ($\frac{1}{8}$ in) along (**D**). Take the needle back in at the end of the previous stitch and out again 3 mm ($\frac{1}{8}$ in) beyond where the thread emerges.

Ladder stitch

This neat handstitch is worked from the right side to match a pattern accurately, or to close an opening left in a seam.

1. Press the seam allowances to the wrong side along the edges to be joined. Butt the edges, matching the pattern if needed.

2. Take the needle along inside the fold of one edge for about 3–6 mm ($\frac{1}{8}$–$\frac{1}{4}$ in). Bring the needle out at the fold, take it directly across to the other fold edge and stitch along inside that fold in the same way (**E**).

STARTING AND FINISHING

A neat, simple way to start and finish handstitching is with one or two backstitches. When tacking, the stitches can be 6 mm ($\frac{1}{4}$ in) long. At other times it is best to make them as small as possible and position them where they are least noticeable. Make the stitch in the same way as the backstitched seam, but make a second stitch on top of the first.

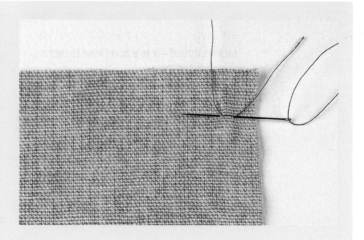

MACHINE-STITCHING

Machine-stitching is quick, accurate and strong. It is well worth mastering the art of finishing ends securely and stitching accurately using the machine guidelines to keep the stitching straight and even.

Reverse stitching

Reverse stitching at the start and finish of a piece of stitching will secure the thread ends, stop the seam from unravelling and avoid the need to hand-finish the ends.

1. Begin stitching about 1.2–1.5 cm ($\frac{1}{2}$–$\frac{5}{8}$ in) in from the end of the seam, positioning the raw edges level with the 1.5 cm ($\frac{5}{8}$ in) guide-line on the plate to the right of the needle.

2. Reverse stitch back to the edge, then stitch forwards along the seam, keeping the seam edges level with the guideline (**F**). Stitch to the ends, then reverse stitch back for the same distance as you did at the beginning.

3. When the stitching is worked around in a circle, overlap the end of the stitching over the beginning by the same amount.

Stitching around corners

Stitch to the corner, stopping 1.5 cm ($\frac{5}{8}$ in) in. Make sure the needle is down – you may need to turn the wheel on your sewing machine by hand. Lift the presser foot, turn the work, check that the new edge is level with the guideline, lower the presser foot and continue along the next edge (**G**).

Stitching around curves

On smooth curves the fabric can be gently guided by hand. On tighter curves, as well as when guiding by hand, stop every few stitches with the needle down, lift the presser foot, turn the work slightly to realign, lower the foot and continue (**H**). Try to stop and turn often when stitching a smooth curve, or you may end up with a series of short, straight lines.

MATCHING PATTERNED FABRICS

When you are joining fabric pieces together, it is often necessary to arrange the fabric so that patterns such as floral designs, checks or stripes match together at the seam. This is particularly important when you are joining large pieces of fabric; for example, when joining two or more widths of fabrics for curtains. Patterned fabrics have a repeat – this is the distance between points where the same part of the design appears again and it is essential to know what this is when calculating fabric amounts, as you will need to allow extra fabric.

1. Press 1.5 cm ($\frac{5}{8}$ in) to the wrong side of the fabric along one edge. This is known as the seam allowance. Lap this edge over the other edge with the fabric facing right side up. Arrange the edges so the pattern matches exactly at the fold edge and pin the two layers together (**I**).

2. Knot the thread end, then, working from the right side, tack the two edges together by taking a stitch in and out of the flat fabric next to the fold, then slipping the needle into and along the fold edge for a short way. Keep the stitches about 1 cm ($\frac{3}{8}$ in) long.

3. Remove the pins and open the fold so the seam can be stitched from the wrong side.

Matching stripes

1. To join stripes lengthways along the seam, arrange the two edges with right sides facing, so the stripes match in the correct sequence along the edge of a stripe.

2. Pin along the edge of the stripe, checking that the pinning is accurate on both sides of the seam (**J**). Tack the seam, removing the pins as you reach them.

1. Stripes can also be matched in the same way as for a pattern. To match stripes at their short ends, arrange the fabric edges with

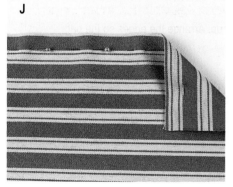

right sides facing, raw edges level and stripes matching.

2. Pin along the edge of a stripe at right angles to the edges, checking that the pinning is accurate on both sides of the seam (**K**). Pin closely and tack over the pins. Machine-stitch, removing the pins as you reach them.

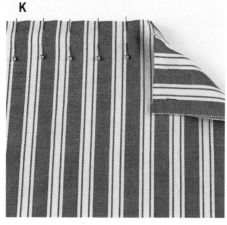

Matching seams

Place the two pieces of fabric together with right sides facing and raw edges level. Match the seams and pin at right angles to the edge, through the actual seam stitching (**L**). Check that the pinning is accurate on both sides. Pin, again at right angles to the edge, along the edges of the seam allowances. Tack over the pins and then machine-stitch, removing the pins you reach them.

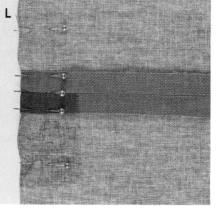

MACHINE-STITCHED SEAMS

Seams join pieces of fabric together and form the basic structure of all sewn items.

Plain seam

A plain seam is quick, neat and long-lasting. Pin and tack the seam as required. Reverse the stitching at each end and stitch the seam along the seamline, using the guides on the machine to keep the stitching evenly spaced in from the edge (**M**).

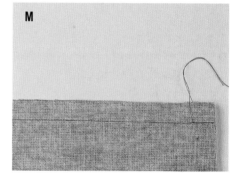

Layering

Layering a seam will reduce the bulk of the seam allowances on thick fabrics to avoid them forming a ridge when they are enclosed within an item. Trim the seam allowance nearest the right side of the item to 1 cm ($\frac{3}{8}$ in), then trim the remaining seam allowance to 6 mm ($\frac{1}{4}$ in) (**N**).

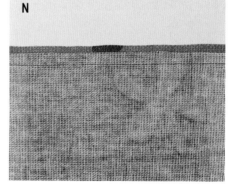

French seam

This is a neat, narrow seam for fine fabrics where the seam may show through.

1. Place the edges together with the raw edge level and the wrong sides facing. Stitch the seam 1 cm ($\frac{3}{8}$ in) in from the edges. Trim the seam allowances to a little less than 6 mm ($\frac{1}{4}$ in) and press them open (**O**).

2. Fold the seam so the right sides are facing and press so the stitching is at the fold edge. Then machine-stitch 6 mm ($\frac{1}{4}$ in) in from the fold edge so the raw edges are enclosed (**P**). Press the seam to one side.

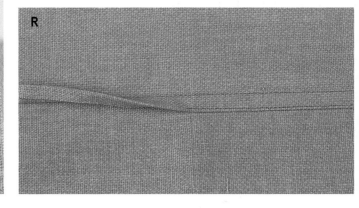

Flat fell or shirt seam

This is a strong, flat seam used to join fabrics where an easy-to-launder seam is required.

1. Place the two edges together with wrong sides facing and raw edges level. Stitch 1.5 cm ($\frac{5}{8}$ in) in from the edge. Trim one seam allowance to 6 mm ($\frac{1}{4}$ in) (**Q**).

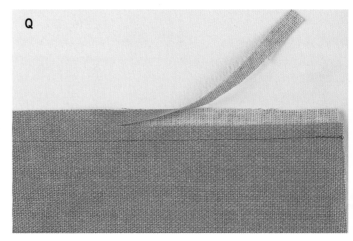

2. Open out the fabric and press the seam so the wider seam allowance lies on top of the trimmed one (**R**). Tuck the wider seam allowance under the trimmed edge and press. Machine-stitch the pressed fold down flat to the fabric. The finished seam will have two rows of machine stitching on the right side.

NEATENING SEAMS

When the edges of your seams are exposed on the wrong side of an item, they may need neatening to prevent the fabric fraying. This can be done by pinking, zigzag stitching or edgestitching.

Pinking

This quick method is useful on fabrics which do not fray easily, such as woollens. Special pinking shears are used to trim away just the very edge of the seam allowance, forming a zigzag shape (**S**).

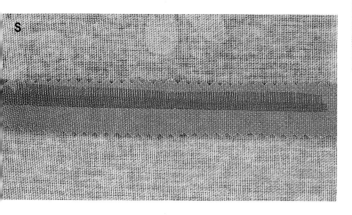

Zigzag stitching

This quick and durable machine method can be worked using an ordinary zigzag stitch, a three-step, or a picot stitch, which has three small stitches formed on each leg of the zigzag. Adjust the stitch to a medium length and medium width zigzag. If the seam is pressed open, zigzag stitch along the edge of each seam allowance separately (**T**). If the edges are pressed together to one side, zigzag stitch the two edges together.

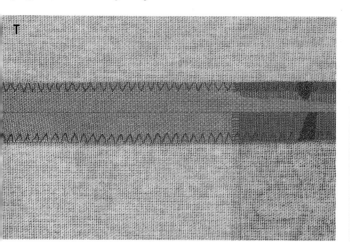

Edgestitching

This machine method is only used on pressed open seams. Fold and press 3 mm (⅛ in) to the wrong side along the edge of each seam allowance. Then, working from the right side, machine straight stitch along the fold through the seam allowance (**U**).

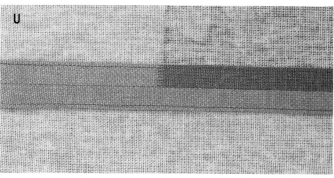

TRIMMING CORNERS

Corners need trimming carefully to prevent the seam allowances inside the corners from being too bulky when the corners are turned right-side out. On square corners, trim diagonally across the corner about 3 mm (⅛ in) outside the stitching at the point of the corner stitching (**V**). Loosely woven or very frayable fabrics will need trimming a little further away from the stitching, while firm, fine fabrics may need trimming a little closer. If the corners are more sharply pointed, trim diagonally first, then trim away another wedge at each side of the corner. Turn corners right-side out by hand, then finish forming the point using a ruler or the closed end of dressmaking shears to gently push the point out. Avoid using anything sharp that could push through the corner.

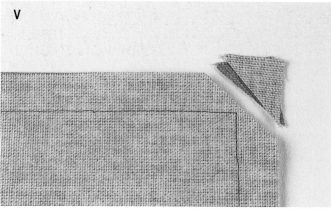

Striped Cushion Covers

Simple seamed fronts add smart designer detail to these easy cushion covers. Strips of silk fabric in a medley of toning shades are stitched together to make a three-colour cover. Striped fabric can also be used to great effect on a cover with diagonal seams. The cover backs are finished with straight hems on an overlapping flap, through which the pad is inserted.

Three-colour cushion

MATERIALS
Pattern paper
Pencil and ruler
$\frac{1}{2}$ m (20 in) silk dupion in three colours
Sewing thread
Cushion pad, 40 cm ($15\frac{3}{4}$ in) square

CUTTING OUT
1 Using the pattern paper, a pencil and a ruler, draw out a pattern 43 cm (17 in) square. Draw lines to divide the pattern into strips that are 23.5 cm ($9\frac{1}{4}$ in)-, 11 cm ($4\frac{1}{2}$ in)- and 8.5 cm ($3\frac{3}{8}$ in)-wide respectively. Cut along the lines, adding 1.5 cm ($\frac{5}{8}$ in) seam allowances to each cut edge.

2 Cut a piece of fabric for the back 63 cm ($26\frac{1}{2}$ in) wide by 43 cm (17 in) long.

STITCHING
1 Stitch the wide and narrow strips to each side edge of the centre strip with a plain seam (**diagram 1**). Press the seams open.

2 Cut the back piece of fabric in half along the 43 cm (17 in) length. Press a 1 cm ($\frac{3}{8}$ in) then a 1.5 cm ($\frac{5}{8}$ in) hem to the wrong side along both cut edges and machine-stitch (**diagram 2**).

DIAGRAM 1   DIAGRAM 2

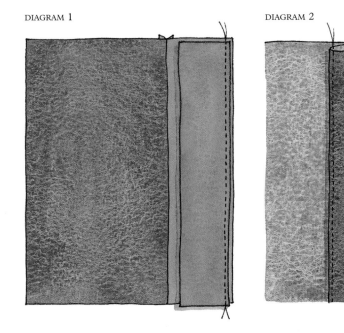

3 With right sides facing, place the back pieces on the front so that the raw edges are level and the hemmed edges overlap. Pin the pieces to hold them together (**diagram 3**). Machine-stitch together around all four edges. Trim the corners and press the seams open as far as possible.

4 Turn the cover right-side out and press the seam at the edge. Insert the cushion pad through the overlapping back edges.

DIAGRAM 3

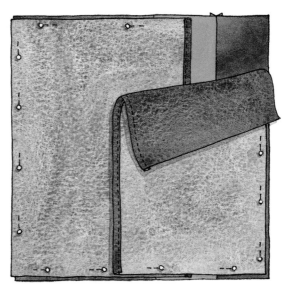

Diagonal Seam Cushion

MATERIALS
Pattern paper
Pencil and ruler
1 m (40 in) medium-weight, striped furnishing fabric
Sewing thread
Cushion pad, 40 cm (15¾ in) square

CUTTING OUT

1 Using the pattern paper, a pencil, and a ruler, draw out a pattern 43 cm (17 in) square. Draw lines diagonally across the square from corner to corner. Cut along the lines and add 1.5 cm (⅝ in) seam allowances to the cut edges on one piece to use as the pattern.

2 Cut out four triangular pieces of fabric, taking care to keep the long edge along the stripe or straight grain of the fabric and to match the stripe accurately on the shorter edges. This is easiest to do if you leave the first piece pinned to the pattern and use that to match the stripes on the next piece. Cut a piece of fabric for the back that is 63 cm (26½ in) wide by 43 cm (17 in) deep.

STITCHING

1 Stitch two triangles together along one of the shorter edges, matching the stripes accurately. Press the seam open. Stitch the other two triangles together in the same way.

2 Place the two large triangles together with the centre seam and stripes matching. Stitch together along the remaining diagonal seam and press the seam open (**diagram 1**). Make the cushion back and complete the cover in the same way as the three-colour cushion.

DIAGRAM 1

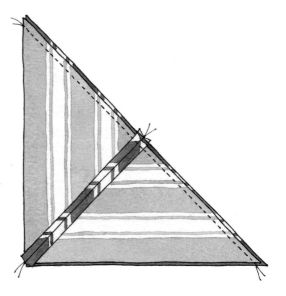

NOTE

For cushion pads that are larger or smaller than those in this project, measure the depth and width of the pad and add on 3 cm (1¼ in) to each measurement for the cushion front. Cut the cushion back to the same depth as the cushion front. To allow for overlap, add 15 cm (6 in) to the front width on cushions up to 35 cm (13¾ in) squared, and 20 cm (8 in) on larger cushions.

Hems

Hems are made to finish off a fabric edge neatly. A hem can be single, where just one layer of fabric is folded to the wrong side, or it can be double, where two layers are folded over. Single hems are used mostly on clothing; double hems are commonly used on soft furnishings.

BASIC HEMS

On a basic hem, just one layer of fabric is folded to the wrong side. Adjust the setting on your sewing machine to a medium-width and -length zigzag stitch and machine-stitch along the raw edge to prevent it from fraying. If the hem is to be covered by a lining, it can be left unneatened. Fold the hem depth to the wrong side and press. Pin, tack and stitch the hem in place by hand or machine (**A**).

The most common type of hem has a small amount of fabric turned to the wrong side, and then the hem depth is folded and pressed again. To hem in this way, first press 1–1.5 cm ($\frac{3}{8}$–$\frac{5}{8}$ in) to the wrong side, then press the hem depth to the wrong side. Pin, tack and stitch in place by hand or machine (**B**). If machine-stitching a single hem, stitch along just below the neatening, or stitch 6 mm ($\frac{1}{4}$ in) in from the edge.

DOUBLE HEM

This type of hem is used on very sheer fabrics to conceal the inner layer of the hem. First press the hem depth to the wrong side, then press the same amount again (**C**). Pin, tack and stitch in place near the top fold. Double hems are usually machine-stitched.

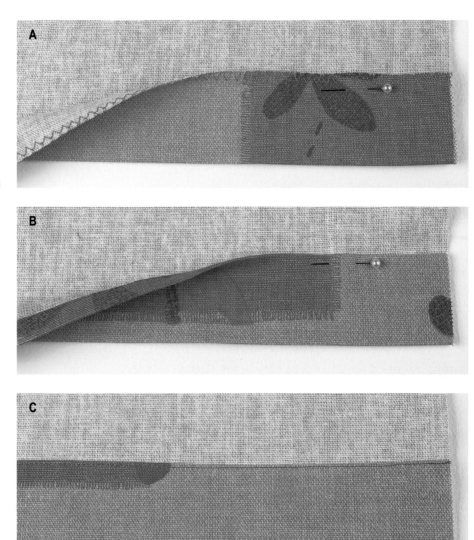

Shortening Trouser Turn-ups

First establish the amount the trouser needs to be shortened, then measure and note the depth of the turn-up. Unpick and fold down the outer part of the turn-up. Measure and note the total depth of the turn-up hem on the inside from the fold to the stitched edge. Unpick the turn-up stitching, open it out and press it flat. Measure, mark and trim away the amount the leg is to be shortened. Press a new turn-up hem to the wrong side to the same measurement as before, then stitch in place. Fold the depth of the turn-up to the right side and then press. Stitch right through the seam line at both the inner and outer leg seams to hold the turn-up in place.

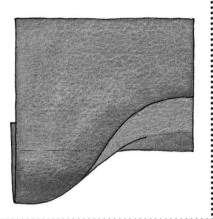

HEMSTITCHED HEM

This neat, hand-stitched finish can be used to stitch both single and double hems. Begin with back stitches near the fold of the hem, then stitch across to pick up just a thread of fabric above the hem (**D**). Stitch along diagonally back again through the hem. Repeat, taking care not to pull too tight.

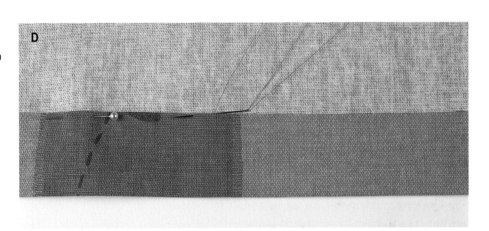

HERRINGBONE STITCH HEM

This handstitched hem is used to stitch single hems, usually on thick, non-fray fabric such as flannel or fleece. The stitching both neatens and stitches the edge so that there is no need to zigzag stitch the edge.

Working from left to right, begin with backstitches. Bring the needle through the hem, take it diagonally up to the right and take a stitch through above the hem from right to left. Bring the needle diagonally down to the right and take a stitch through the hem, again from right to left (**E**). Repeat, taking care not to pull too tight.

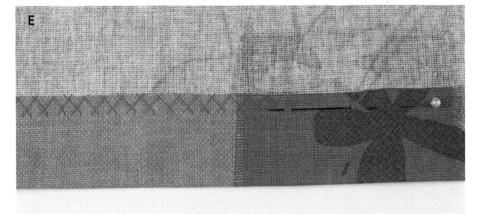

MACHINE-ROLLED HEM

This neat hem is easy to make once you get started, but the beginning can be a bit messy, so it's worth allowing extra fabric to discard. Most machines come with a roll-hem foot that has a small metal scroll at the front that rolls and forms the hem prior to stitching.

1. Fix the roll-hem foot to the machine. At the hem's start, fold and press a double 3 mm (⅛ in) hem to the wrong side for 8 cm (3 in).

2. Lower the foot onto the hem and stitch a few stitches while holding the bobbin threads at the back. Lower the needle and raise the presser foot. Unfold the pressed hem and guide it onto the scroll. Lower the foot and begin stitching (**F**), lifting the fabric edge and guiding it onto the scroll as you go.

F

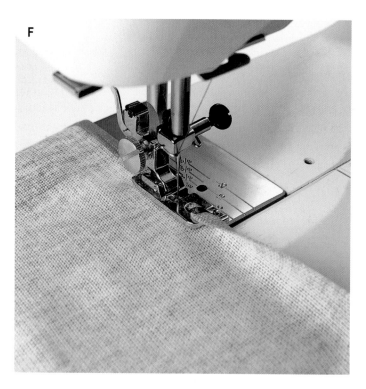

Hem alterations

SHORTENING

When shortening a garment, mark the new hem level with pins and measure the amount by which you intend to shorten the garment. Unpick the existing hem using small scissors or an unpicker, cut the thread, then open the hem out and press it flat. Measure the amount to be shortened in from the edge and mark it at intervals all around with an eraseable fabric marker pen. Trim away the fabric along the marked line so the hem allowance left is the same as the first hem. Refold the hem and stitch in place.

LENGTHENING

Unpick the existing hem using small scissors or an unpicker, cut the thread, then open the hem out and press it flat. Refold the new, shorter hem to the wrong side and stitch in place. If the original hem line is worn or faded, stitch a narrow braid or ribbon over it. If a single row looks odd, add another row to make it into a decorative feature. On children's clothes, where the garment may soon need lengthening again, allow twice the hem amount and fold a double hem to allow fabric for lengthening later.

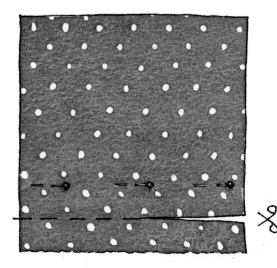

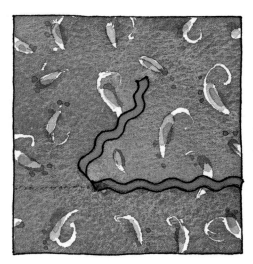

CURVED HEM

On curved hems the extra fullness can be eased in by one of two methods.

1. On a gentle curve, such as around a circular tablecloth, machine-stitch around the fold of the hem 1.5 cm ($\frac{5}{8}$ in) in from the edge.

2. Using the point of an iron, press the hem over to the wrong side, rolling it over to form a smooth curve. Tuck under the inner edge of the hem to make a 1 cm ($\frac{3}{8}$ in) hem, then pin, tack and machine-stitch in place (**G**).

1. On tighter curves, stitch around the opened out inner fold of the hem with a gathering stitch. Pull up the thread to ease the fullness (**H**). Arrange the fullness evenly, then pin, tack and machine-stitch in place.

G

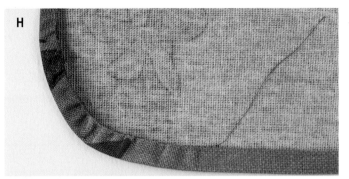

H

LENGTHENING WITH BIAS BINDING

On items being lengthened as far as possible, the edge can be finished with bias binding. Unpick and unfold the hem and press it flat. Unfold one edge of the binding and place it, right sides facing, to the hem edge so that the raw edges are level. Stitch in place along the crease of the binding (**A**), then fold the binding to the wrong side so that it forms the hem (**B**). Stitch in place.

BINDING A HEM

This method uses bias binding to finish a lengthened hem, but in this method the binding shows as a narrow border along the edge. If you cannot get a good match in the binding, choose a contrasting colour. If the original hemline shows, a strip of folded binding could be stitched over the line to hide it (**A**). Unpick and unfold the hem, then press it flat. Unfold one edge of the binding and place it, right sides facing, to the hem edge so that the raw edges are level (**B**). Stitch in place along the crease of the binding, then fold just the edge of the binding over to the wrong side. Handstitch to the back of the first row of stitching.

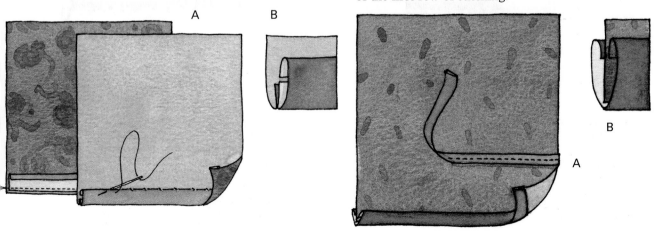

A   B

B

A

Tie Top Curtains

Simple but effective, tie top curtains are some of the easiest window dressings to make. For this project we have chosen satin ribbon for the ties, which are inserted neatly between each curtain and the facing strip that finishes the top edges of the curtains.

MATERIALS
Fabric of your choice
Sewing thread
Ribbon, 1.5 cm ($\frac{5}{8}$ in) wide, 40 cm (16 in) per tie

CUTTING OUT

1 Cut the fabric to the required length plus 11 cm ($4\frac{1}{4}$ in) by the required width, plus 4 cm ($1\frac{1}{2}$ in) for hems, plus a fullness allowance (see below). Cut a separate 7 cm ($2\frac{3}{4}$ in)-deep facing strip the same width as the curtains.

Fabrics and Fullness

Lightweight voiles and lawns are ideal for floaty tie top curtains, though linens and cottons can also work well if you require a denser window covering.

The amount of fullness to add when making curtains is really a matter of personal preference. You could make your curtains flat, so they just cover the window area when closed, but they usually look better with a little fullness. Add about 20 cm (8 in) per metre for a gentle fullness, or up to half the width again for a more gathered look. You could even allow twice the window width for a very opulent look. Try holding your fabric up and gathering it in your hands to ascertain how much fullness you prefer.

STITCHING

1 Press 1 cm ($\frac{3}{8}$ in) then another 1 cm ($\frac{3}{8}$ in) to the wrong side along the edges of each curtain to make a double hem. Machine-stitch in place.

2 Cut a 40 cm (15 $\frac{3}{4}$ in) length of ribbon for each tie and press the ties in half. Mark the positions for the ties on the right side of the curtains, one at the edge of each curtain, then space the others evenly between about 15 cm (6 in) apart. Pin and tack the ties in place so that they hang downwards and the fold is level with the top edge (**diagram 1**).

DIAGRAM 1

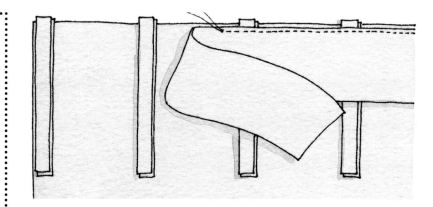

3 With right sides facing and the top raw edges level, place the facing over the ties, allowing it to project at each end. Stitch the facing in place 1 cm ($\frac{3}{8}$ in) down from the top edges of the curtains.

4 Trim the side edges of the facing 1 cm (³⁄₈ in) outside each curtain. Press the facing away from the curtains and press 1 cm (³⁄₈ in) to the wrong side around the remaining raw edges. Press the facing over to the wrong side of each curtain and machine-stitch in place along the side and lower edges (**diagram 2**). Then, if desired, machine-stitch along the top edge on the right side.

5 Press 5 cm (2 in) and then another 5 cm (2 in) to the wrong side across the lower edge of each curtain and machine-stitch in place.

DIAGRAM 2

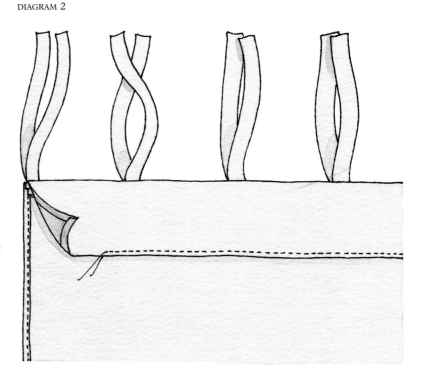

Curtain alterations

Give curtains that are too short for a new window a new lease on life with stylish border panels at the bottom and leading edges of the curtains. Broad panels stitched across the base add the required length, and the narrow vertical borders tie the new fabric in with the rest of the curtain. To join the old fabric with the new, unpick the curtain hems and trim the hem away along the hem fold line. Cut the new border twice the required depth, plus seam allowances. Stitch the border to the right side of the curtains, then fold half the depth to the wrong side and handstitch in place on the inside (**A**). Stitch the narrow border to the lead edges of the curtains in the same way.

A

Child's Apron

This useful child's apron has curved hems and a pocket. The straps for the waist ties and head loop have been made from the same fabric as the apron itself, but tape or ribbon could be also be used. The dimensions of this apron make it suitable for a child aged 4–7.

MATERIALS

Pattern paper
Pencil and ruler
1 m (40 in) cotton fabric
Sewing thread

CUTTING OUT

1 Draw a line 19 cm (7½ in) long across for the top edge of the apron, then draw a line 60 cm (23½ in) down the centre to mark the length (**diagram 1**). Mark 21 cm (8¼ in) down from the top on the centre line, then measure 22 cm (8¾ in) out from either side of the mark to mark the side edges. Draw in the side and lower edges, joining them with curves at the lower corners. Then draw curved lines to join the top corners to the side edges to form the apron shape.

2 Draw out a pocket pattern 23 cm (9 in) wide by 15 cm (6 in) deep with a curved lower edge. Fold the patterns in half and cut out to ensure that both halves are symmetrical. Cut out the apron and pocket. Cut three straps 53 cm (21 in) by 6 cm (2¼ in) (if using fabric).

DIAGRAM 1

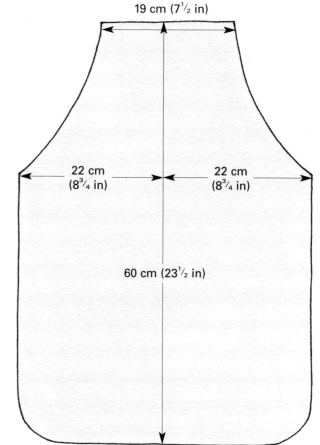

19 cm (7½ in)

22 cm (8¾ in)   22 cm (8¾ in)

60 cm (23½ in)

STITCHING

1 Press 1 cm ($\frac{3}{8}$ in), then another 1 cm ($\frac{3}{8}$ in) to the wrong side on the curved side edges on the bib of the apron and machine-stitch in place.

2 Sew a gathering stitch around the lower corners 1 cm ($\frac{3}{8}$ in) in from the edge. Press double 1 cm ($\frac{3}{8}$ in) hems to the wrong side around the side and lower edges, pulling up the gathering stitching to ease the fullness evenly. Machine-stitch in place.

3 Stitch a row of machine stitching around 1.5 cm ($\frac{5}{8}$ in) in from the curved edge of the pocket. Using the stitching as a guide, press the seam allowance over to the wrong side so that the stitching just rolls over onto the wrong side.

4 Press 1 cm ($\frac{3}{8}$ in), then 2 cm ($\frac{3}{4}$ in) hems to the wrong side across the top of the apron and the top of the pocket, then machine-stitch in place.

5 Press the pocket in half to mark its centre. Place the pocket to the apron with its top edge 23 cm (9 in) down from the top of the apron. Machine-stitch in place around the curved edges and down the centre, following the crease as a guide.

6 Press 1 cm ($\frac{3}{8}$ in) to the wrong side around all edges of the straps, then press the straps in half lengthways and stitch along the length and across the ends. Underlap the ends of one strap under the hem at each side of the apron and stitch in place with a square of stitching. Stitch the other two straps to the top of the side edges in the same way (**diagram 2**).

DIAGRAM 2

NOTE

Aprons can suffer a great deal of wear and tear. To repair an L-shaped tear, cut a piece of matching or toning fabric about 1 cm ($^3/_8$ in) bigger all around than the tear. Place the fabric behind the tear and tack around the outer edge. Stitch in place with a close three-step zigzag stitch worked along the tear. On a larger tear, machine-stitch first forwards, then in reverse, to-and-fro across the tear to form a close zigzag formation. When complete, trim the excess patch from the wrong side.

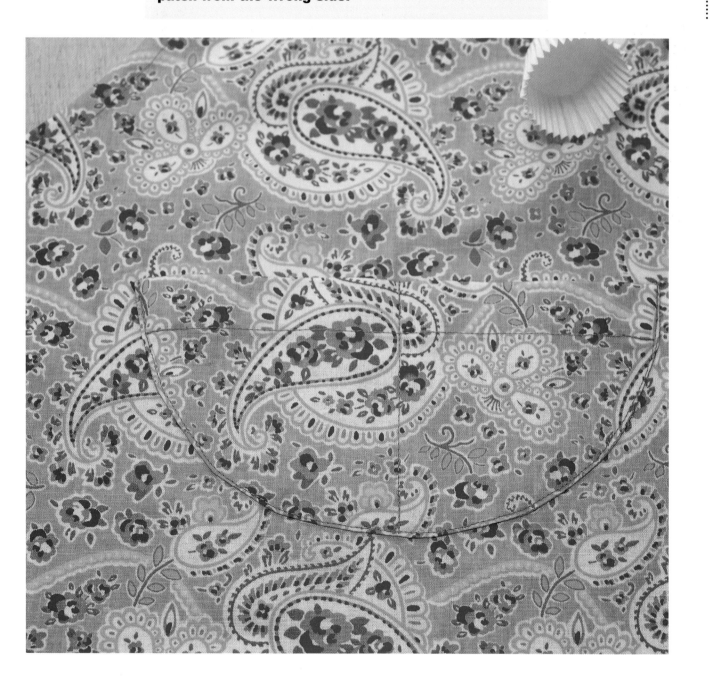

Curved Seams and Binding

Sometimes a project demands that the fabric edge needs more than a simple straight seam. Curved seams are stitched in the same way as plain straight seams but they need trimming and snipping after the seam is stitched. Binding is a neat and decorative way to finish a fabric edge.

CURVED SEAMS

Most curved seams will ease into shape more smoothly, particularly on small items, if the seam allowances are first trimmed to about half their original width. The trimmed seam then needs to be snipped or notched.

Snipping into seams

On concave curves, such as the inside of a circle, snip into the seam allowance so the seam allowance can expand when turned right-side out (**A**). On convex curves such as the outside of a circle, cut out small wedge-shaped notches. The tighter the curve, the closer together the notches and snips should be.

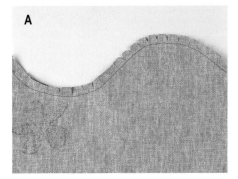

A

Scallops

Scalloped edges are often finished with a facing. This is a separate piece of fabric cut to the scalloped shape, but a bit deeper than the scallops. Stitch the facing to the scalloped edge with curved seams, then trim and notch the seam allowances as before. Also snip into the seam allowance at the top point between each scallop to just a couple of threads outside the stitching. Turn the scalloped edge right-side out and press the seam at the edge (**B**).

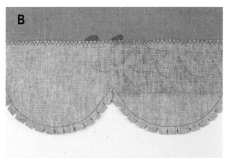

B

Topstitching

Topstitching is decorative stitching that is worked on the right side of the fabric, usually to outline an edge (**C**). It also often serves a functional purpose by creating a firmer edge or keeping a facing in place on the inside.

Topstitching can be worked near the edge of a fabric or a little way in. To keep the stitching even, use the guides on your sewing machine to keep the edge being topstitched level with the inner or outer edge of the presser foot so the stitching remains the same distance away throughout.

When you are topstitching a curved edge, work around the curve, stopping with the needle down every few stitches and turning the fabric slightly in the same way as you would when stitching a curved seam.

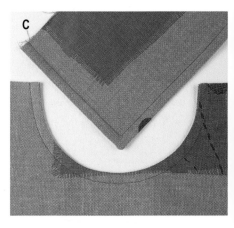

C

BINDING

Binding gives a neat finish to a fabric edge. The binding can be plain, to make a smart outline, or it can be checked or patterned to make a pretty edging. Bias binding can be purchased ready-made, or it can be made from bias strips. Ready-made bias binding is available in various widths – the finished binding will be half the width of the purchased binding.

Making bias binding

To make your own bias binding, cut long strips of fabric four times the required finished width diagonally across the fabric. This is called cutting on the bias. Then press both long edges in so that they almost meet at the centre (**D**).

Joining bias strips

This neat method is used when it is necessary to join fabric cut bias strips to make up the length required.

1. Open out the binding folds. If required, trim the two ends on the straight grain. Place the two ends together with right sides facing, straight ends level and the foldlines intersecting 6 mm ($\frac{1}{4}$ in) in. Pin to hold.

2. Stitch the two ends together, taking a 6 mm ($\frac{1}{4}$ in) seam (**E**). Open out the binding and press the seam open.

3. Trim off the corners of the seam level with the edge of the binding and re-press the binding folds.

Binding an edge

1. Unfold one edge of the binding and place the raw edge level with the fabric edge on the right side of the fabric. Machine-stitch in place along the fold (**F**).

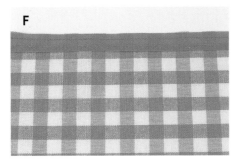

2. Fold the other edge of the binding over to the wrong side (so its edge is level with the machine-stitching) and stitch in place by hand (**G**).

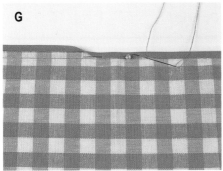

Joining ends

There are two ways of joining the ends of two binding strips. The first is to join the ends with a diagonal seam before the stitching is complete. An alternative, easier method is to overlap the finishing end over the starting end, tuck the raw end under, then complete the stitching (**H**).

Binding an edge: machine method

First unfold one edge of the binding and place the raw edge level with the fabric edge on the wrong side of the fabric. Machine stitch in place along the fold. Fold the other edge of the binding over to the right side so its edge just covers the previous stitching and machine-stitch in place (**I**).

Binding an edge: sandwich method

Before stitching, fold and press the binding in half lengthways so the upper half, which will be on the right side, is slightly narrower than the lower half. Sandwich the fabric into the binding and machine-stitch in place from the left side (**J**).

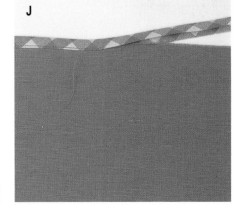

Peg Bag

This handy bag, ideal for laundry pegs, has
a rounded opening at the front which can
be finished with either a simple facing or
smart binding. A wooden coat hanger, slipped
inside the top edges, suspends the bag from a
door hook or washing line.

MATERIALS
Wooden coat hanger
Pattern paper
Pencil and ruler
1 m (40 in) furnishing fabric
Sewing thread

DIAGRAM 1

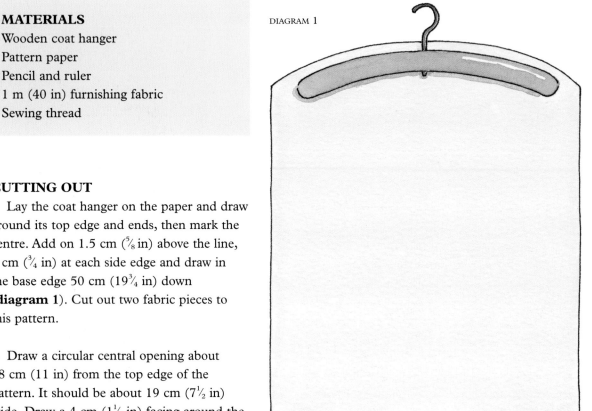

CUTTING OUT

1 Lay the coat hanger on the paper and draw
around its top edge and ends, then mark the
centre. Add on 1.5 cm ($\frac{5}{8}$ in) above the line,
2 cm ($\frac{3}{4}$ in) at each side edge and draw in
the base edge 50 cm (19$\frac{3}{4}$ in) down
(**diagram 1**). Cut out two fabric pieces to
this pattern.

2 Draw a circular central opening about
28 cm (11 in) from the top edge of the
pattern. It should be about 19 cm (7$\frac{1}{2}$ in)
wide. Draw a 4 cm (1$\frac{1}{2}$ in) facing around the
opening. Cut out the opening for the front of
the bag from one piece of fabric. Trace off the
facing pattern and cut this out from the
fabric.

STITCHING

DIAGRAM 2

1 Zigzag stitch around the outer edge of the facing to neaten. Place the facing to the opening with right sides facing, and stitch in place around the opening, taking a 1 cm ($^3/_8$ in) seam allowance. Snip and notch the seam allowances around the curves and press the facing over to the wrong side. Topstitch around the facing 1 cm ($^3/_8$ in) in from the edge.

2 Place the front piece to the back piece with right sides facing and outer edges level. Stitch together around the outer edges (**diagram 2**). Notch the seam at the curves and trim the corners. Turn the bag right-side out and press the seam to the edge. Slip the coat hanger inside the top edge to hang the peg bag.

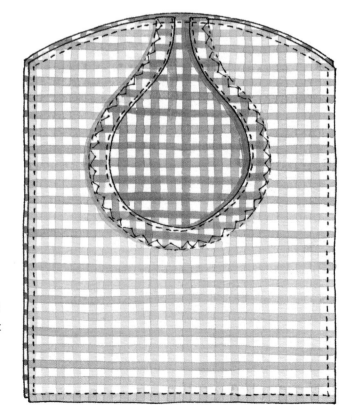

Bound Edge Alternative

An alternative to facing the opening, bias binding gives a neat contrast outline around the opening. As bias binding is always cut on the bias or crossways grain of the fabric, it should mould easily to sit smoothly around the curves. The binding shown here was first machine-stitched to the right side. The other edge was then folded over to the wrong side and hand-stitched in place using the method shown on page 35.

Casings

Casings form channels, usually at the top of a bag or the waist of a garment, through which cord, ribbon or elastic is threaded to draw in the garment. Casings can also be made at the top of curtains to thread a pole or rod through. The casing can be sewn at the edge of the fabric, or it can be positioned just in from the edge, so that a frill forms above when it is drawn up. A casing can also be cut from a separate strip of fabric.

FOLD-OVER CASINGS

This simple casing provides a channel to thread through cord or elastic. It is useful for making simple drawstring bags and waistbands.

1. First press 1 cm (³⁄₈ in) to the wrong side, then press the depth of the casing to the wrong side. Pin and tack in place (**A**).

2. Machine-stitch in place along the lower edge (**B**). You can also stitch a second row of machine-stitching around the top of the casing to give it a neat finish.

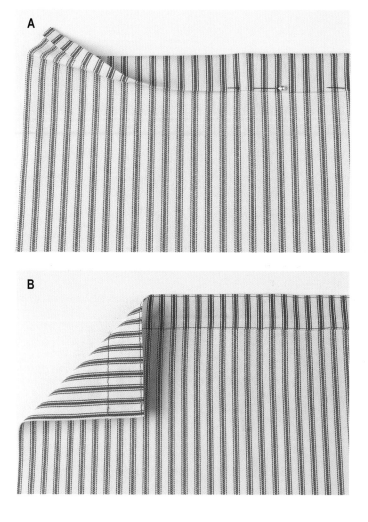

A

B

SELF-FRILL CASINGS

This type of casing is similar to the fold-over casing, but here the channels are stitched in from the edge so that a frill of fabric stands up above the casing.

1. First press 1 cm ($\frac{3}{8}$ in) to the wrong side, then press the depth of the casing plus the depth of the frill over to the wrong side (**C**). Pin, tack, then machine-stitch in place along the lower edge of the casing.

2. Stitch a second row about 2–3 cm ($\frac{3}{4}$–$1\frac{1}{4}$ in) above the first to form the casing channel (**D**).

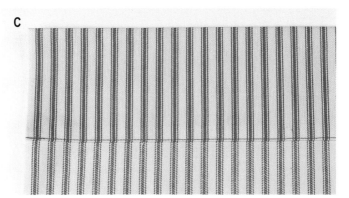

SEPARATE CASINGS

These casings have a separate strip cut to form the casing. The strip can be cut straight, or on the bias if it is to fit around a curved edge. Cut the strip the required depth of the casing plus 2 cm ($\frac{3}{4}$ in) on the length and 2.5 cm (1 in) on the width.

1. Press 1 cm ($\frac{3}{8}$ in) to the wrong side at the two short ends and lower long edge of the casing strip. Place the casing to the edge of the garment with right sides facing and raw edges level. Pin, tack, then stitch in place 1.5 cm ($\frac{5}{8}$ in) in from the edge of the garment (**E**).

2. Press the casing over to the wrong side. Pin, tack and machine-stitch in place around the lower edge of the strip (**F**). Stitch a second row around just below the top edge to give it a neat finish.

Drawstring Bag

Ideal for shoes, underwear, or toys, this
drawstring bag has a casing at the top edge,
with a channel stitched down from the edge to
form a self-frill at the top when the bag is
pulled closed.

MATERIALS

½ m (20 in) furnishing fabric
Sewing thread
2 m (2¼ yds) ribbon or cord

CUTTING OUT

1 Cut out two fabric pieces, both 35 cm
(13¾ in) wide x 50 cm (19¾ in) deep.

STITCHING

1 Place the two pieces of fabric together with
right sides facing and raw edges level. Mark a
2 cm (¾ in) gap about 14–16 cm (5½–6¼ in)
down from the top on both sides. This will
allow for the side openings. Stitch the two
pieces of fabric together around the side and
base edges. Trim the corners and press the
seams open.

NOTE

**Ribbons and cords both make
quick and easy drawstrings for a
bag. Shoelaces could even be
used to make a sporty shoe bag!
To insert a ribbon into a casing,
thread the ribbon onto a large-
eyed, blunt needle, then pass the
needle along through the casing
to thread the ribbon in place.
Alternatively, fasten a safety pin
onto the end of a ribbon or cord
and use it to hold onto while
threading the casing around.**

2 Press 1 cm (⅜ in) to the wrong side
around the top edge, then press 7.5 cm (3 in)
over to the wrong side to form the casing.
Stitch around the lower edge of the casing,
then again 2 cm (¾ in) above the first row to
form the casing channel (**diagram 1**).

DIAGRAM 1

3 Turn the bag right-side out and press the
seams at the edges. Cut the ribbon or cord
into two equal lengths. Thread one length in
through one side opening through the casing
channel and back out the same opening.
Knot the ends together. Thread the other
length through the opposite opening in the
same way.

Mitred Corners and Borders

Mitring is a neat way to remove fullness from the corners on seams and hems. The mitres can be formed and left unstitched to make neat corners on pocket seams, or they can be stitched, as they often are on deeper hems.

MITRING A CORNER

Press the seam allowance or hem to the wrong side on the two sides adjacent to the corner, then unfold the edges. Fold the corner in diagonally across the point where the two folds intersect and press (**A**). Trim the corner 1 cm ($\frac{3}{8}$ in) in from the fold and refold the mitre. Unstitched mitres on fine fabrics can be trimmed closer.

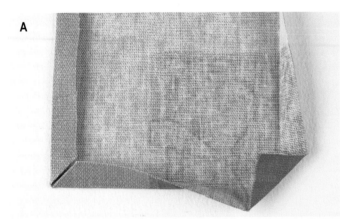

A

Stitching a mitred corner

Form the mitred corner as above and hand-stitch the mitred edges together along the pressed crease using a ladder stitch (**B**).

B

Double-mitred hem

1. Press the appropriate double hem in place, then unfold the outer fold. Fold the corner over diagonally, level with the inner pressed corner (**C**). Press the fold and trim the corner away 1 cm ($\frac{3}{8}$ in) inside the fold.

C

2. Refold the corners so the pressed lines match. Stitch along the pressed line from the corner to finish at the outer hem fold. Press the mitre seam open (**D**). Refold the hem and press again. Alternatively, the formed mitre can be ladder-stitched like the mitred corner.

D

DOUBLE-MITRED BORDER

1. Fold the borders in half with the wrong sides outside. Overlap the ends of two borders at right angles, with the fold edges on the outer edges and the ends, projecting by 1.5 cm ($\frac{5}{8}$ in), and pin. Draw a seam line diagonally across the corner between the points where the borders intersect (**E**).

E

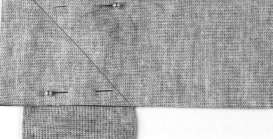

2. Mark the seam allowance 1 cm ($\frac{3}{8}$ in) outside the seam line. Turn the border over and repeat on the other side. Trim along the outer lines (**F**).

F

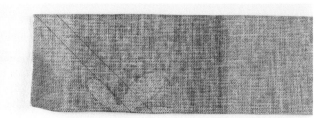

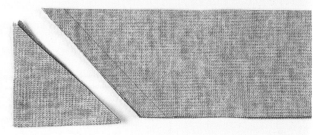

3. Unpin the borders, open them out and mark the seamline on the unmarked half of each border. Place the appropriate two borders together with right sides facing and stitch along the marked lines, starting and finishing 1.5 cm ($\frac{5}{8}$ in) in from the side edges of the border (**G**).

G

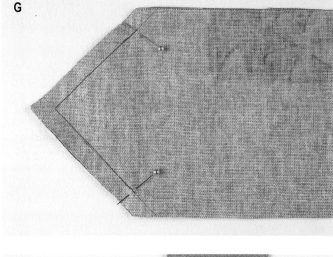

4. Trim the point and press the seam open. Stitch all four corners in this way. Turn the border right-side out. Fold the border in half with the wrong sides facing and press (**H**).

H

Tablecloth and Napkin

A gingham border adds a smart finishing touch to this pretty floral tablecloth and four matching napkins. The mitred double border is stitched first to the wrong side then to the right side, enclosing all the raw edges inside the border. This gives a neat finish and makes the garment strong enough for frequent laundering.

MATERIALS

Cotton fabric (for tablecloth and napkin panels)
Gingham fabric (for tablecloth and napkin borders)
Sewing thread

CUTTING OUT

1 Cut out the cotton tablecloth fabric to the required finished size minus 13 cm ($5\frac{1}{8}$ in) (seam allowances of 1.5 cm ($\frac{5}{8}$ in) are included). Cut the four gingham fabric borders the length of the cloth sides plus 16 cm ($6\frac{1}{4}$ in) x 19 cm ($7\frac{1}{4}$ in) wide.

2 Cut the eight napkin panels 34 cm ($13\frac{1}{2}$ in) square and the four gingham borders 44 x 13 cm ($17\frac{1}{4}$ x $5\frac{1}{8}$ in).

STITCHING

1 Make the tablecloth first. Stitch the short edges of the tablecloth borders together to make a double-mitred border (see page 45).

2 Mark the centre of each edge of the cloth and the border with pins. Place one edge of the border to the wrong side of the cloth and pin together at the centre pin with the raw edges level.

3 Match and pin at the corners so the end of the mitre stitching is 1.5 cm ($\frac{5}{8}$ in) in from the edge of the cloth at each corner (**diagram 1**). Pin between the corners and centre pins and then tack. Stitch the border in place, stopping and restarting at each corner.

4 Press 1.5 cm ($\frac{5}{8}$ in) to the wrong side around the edges of the remaining border and place this edge onto the right side of the cloth so all the raw edges are enclosed. Pin, tack, then machine-stitch in place on the right side (**diagram 2**). The finished border will be 8 cm ($3\frac{1}{4}$ in) wide.

5 Make the napkins in the same way as the tablecloth. The napkin borders will be 5 cm (2 in) wide.

DIAGRAM 2

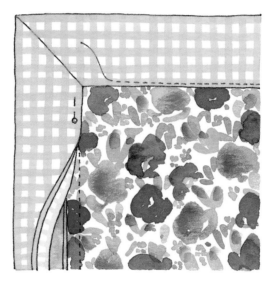

DIAGRAM 1

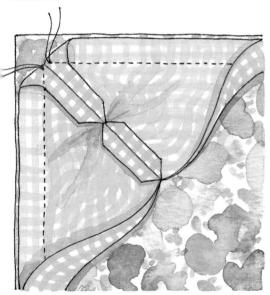

Table Runner with Mitred Border

This silk table runner has an organza mitred border, making it a gorgeous centrepiece for any table. The measurements given will make a runner with a 26 cm (10$\frac{1}{4}$ in)-wide centre panel with 7 cm (2$\frac{3}{4}$ in) borders.

MATERIALS

Silk dupion fabric for centre panel
(amount as required)
Organza fabric (amount as required)
Erasable marker pen
Ruler
Sewing thread

CUTTING OUT

1 To estimate the length of the centre panel, measure the total length of the table and subtract 11 cm (4$\frac{1}{4}$ in). Cut out two central panels 29 cm (11$\frac{1}{2}$ in) wide by the required length. Allow 1.5 cm ($\frac{5}{8}$ in) for seams.

2 For the short ends of the border, cut organza strips 17 cm (6$\frac{3}{4}$ in) wide by 43 cm (17 in). Cut organza strips for the long edges the same width and by the cut length of the centre panel plus 14 cm (5$\frac{1}{2}$ in).

STITCHING

1 Stitch the borders together to form a long, rectangular double-mitred border (**diagram 1**) (see page 45 for making double-mitred borders).

DIAGRAM 1

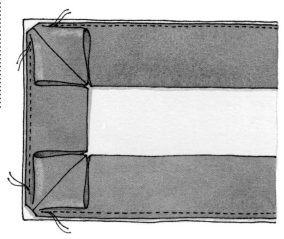

2 Treating the two layers of the border as one, mark the centre of the raw border edges and the edges of one centre panel with pins. With right sides facing and raw edges level, place the border around the edge of one centre panel. Match and pin to join the border and panel in the centre.

3 Match and pin at the corners so the end of the mitre stitching is 1.5 cm ($\frac{5}{8}$ in) from the edges of the panel at each corner. Pin between the corners and centre pins, then tack. Stitch the border in place, stopping and restarting the stitching neatly at each corner.

4 Press 1.5 cm ($\frac{5}{8}$ in) to the wrong side around the edges of the remaining centre panel piece. Place to the wrong side of the stitched panel so that its edges are level with the previous stitching and all raw edges are enclosed. Handstitch in place into the back of the previous stitching (**diagram 2**).

DIAGRAM 2

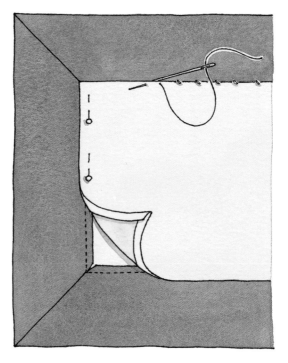

Table Runner with Two Borders

Coordinated country checks and stripes make a chic table runner with a double-mitred border. Cut the centre panel 25 cm (10 in) narrower than the width you require for the finished runner, and cut the first single borders to the length of the panel edges plus 14 x 10 cm (5½ x 4 in). Stitch the single borders to the centre panel, finishing the stitching 1.5 cm (⅝ in) in from each corner. One by one, fold each corner diagonally so the two borders are level. Draw the mitre line across the border in line with the diagonal fold on the centre panel. Stitch the borders together along the line, trim away the excess fabric, then stitch on the outer double-mitred border.

Fastenings

Zips, buttons and other fastenings join edges together in a temporary way so an item can be opened and refastened easily. While fastenings serve an obvious functional purpose, many can also be used for decorative effect.

ZIPS

Zips are available in a range of colours and sizes, and also in different weights. Zip lengths are sized at 5 cm (2 in) intervals. The zip length refers to the length of the zip teeth. Most zips will have extra zip tape protruding beyond the teeth at each end for stitching a neat finish. There are a number of different types of zips:

Chain zip The standard medium-weight, multipurpose zip with plastic or metal teeth on a woven tape.

Coil zip A lightweight zip with the opening part formed by nylon or polyester coils attached to a woven tape.

Concealed zip A specialist type of coil zip with the coiled teeth concealed behind the zip tape. These zips can only be inserted using a concealed zip machine foot.

Open-ended zips A heavyweight zip with metal or plastic teeth that can be separated at the base to form two halves.

Positioning zips in seams

Zips placed in seams will have a seam continuing at each end of the zip. This method is used mainly on cushion covers.

1. Stitch with a plain seam, leaving an opening the length of the zip teeth plus 6 mm ($\frac{1}{4}$ in) (**A**).

2. Press the seam open, continuing to press the seam allowances to the wrong side along the open part in preparation for inserting the zip. When inserting the zip, arrange it centrally within the opening.

A

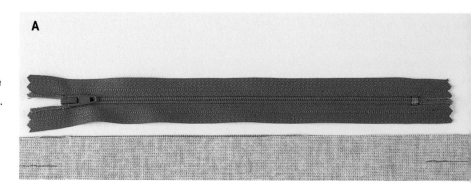

Positioning zips in waistbands

Zips that finish into waistbands have a seam at the lower ends of the zip only, and can open at the top.

1. Stitch with a plain seam first, leaving an opening the length of the zip teeth plus 2 cm ($\frac{3}{4}$ in) for the seam allowance at the waist edge (**B**).

2. Press the seam open, continuing to press the seam allowances to the wrong side along the open part in preparation for inserting the zip. When inserting the zip, arrange the lower end of the zip teeth at the base of the opening.

B

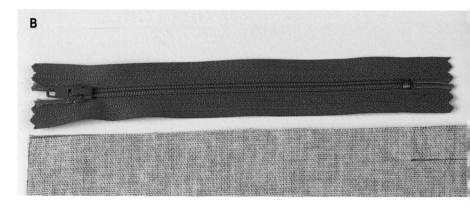

Inserting a lapped zip

A lapped zip has one fabric edge lapped over to cover the zip. This method can be used for positioning a lapped zip in a seam as well as into a waistband.

1. Working with right sides uppermost, pin and tack the zip behind the opening so the right-hand edge of the opening is just outside the zip teeth. Using a zip machine foot, stitch in place near the edge. Begin stitching with the zip partway open, then stop with the needle down, slide the zipper past the needle and complete the stitching (**C**).

2. Arrange the other edge of the opening level with the stitching. Pin, then tack this edge about 1 cm ($\frac{3}{8}$ in) in from the zip tape. Stitch along the long edge again, starting with the zip partway open in the same way as with the first edge. At the end of the zip, stitch across at an angle to finish neatly (**D**).

Exposed zip

This easy method exposes the zip teeth and some of the tape for a decorative effect. No stitching is visible on the right side. This method is only suitable for joining two separate edges that are not seamed together at either end of the zip. Arrange the zip centrally on the fabric edge, with the right sides facing and the zip tape nearest the fabric edge. Pin and tack the zip tape to the fabric 1.5 cm ($\frac{5}{8}$ in) in from the edge. Machine-stitch in place. Stitch the other edge of the fabric to the other edge of the zip in the same way.

BUTTONS

There are two main types of buttons: flat buttons, which have two or four holes pierced through them from the front to the back, and shank buttons, which are stitched on by a protruding shank at the back. A shank spaces the button away from the fabric to allow fabric layers to lie flat under the button when it is fastened. The thicker the fabric, the longer the shank needs to be. Stitch buttons on with doubled thread for strength.

Stitching on flat buttons

To sew on a button with two holes, fasten it onto the fabric with a few backstitches on the wrong side. Bring the needle up through one hole in the button, then back down the other hole and through the fabric. Work four to six stitches in this way to secure, then fasten off with backstitches behind the button. On buttons with four holes, work two parallel sets of stitches (**E**), or form the stitches into a cross.

Making a shank for a flat button

1. Stitch on the button in the same way as for a button with holes, but stitch over a toothpick or a thick needle placed on top of the button as a spacer (**F**).

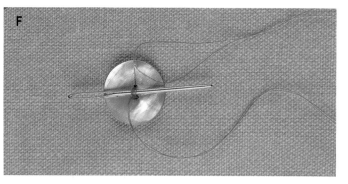

2. Before finishing off, take the thread through between the button and the fabric. Remove the spacer and wind the thread around the stitches between the button and fabric to form a thread shank (**G**). Fasten off.

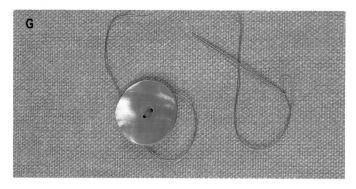

Stitching on a shank button

Fasten the thread on the fabric with a few backstitches on the wrong side. Stitch alternately through the shank and the fabric four to six times, then fasten off with backstitches on the wrong side behind the button (**H**).

Fabric-covered buttons

Plastic and metal moulds for making your own covered buttons are available in kit form.

1. To cover a button, first cut out a circle of fabric to the size given on the button packet. Stitch a small running stitch around the edge of the circle. Place the button front onto the fabric circle and pull up the running stitches to gather the circle in (**I**).

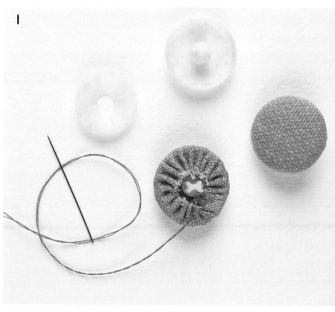

2. Arrange the fabric so that the button is covered smoothly, fasten off the thread and push the button back onto the front to clip the two pieces together.

Some types of covered buttons do not need gathering; these have little metal hooks inside the rim of the button mould. Pull the edge of the fabric circle onto the hooks first on two opposite edges, then onto the other two opposite edges. Then, unhooking and rehooking when necessary, hook on the areas in between. When the circle is fastened in place, smoothly clip the back on.

MAKING BUTTONHOLES

Buttonholes are quick and easy to make using a sewing machine. The exact method varies according to the machine model and will be explained in the machine's manual.

Buttonholes are stitched with a close zigzag stitch, with a wide stitch at each end called a bar tack, and stitches half as wide along each side of the buttonhole (**J**). To establish the length of the buttonhole, add the depth of the button to its diameter. Always make a test buttonhole on spare fabric first to test the size.

Cut the buttonhole along the centre after stitching using small scissors. Cut from each end toward the centre.

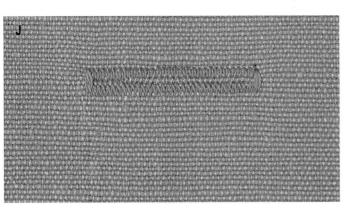

Handstitched buttonholes

Handstitched buttonholes are usually made with one round end, where the button will sit, and one square end. If the holes are being made for ribbon or cord slots, they can be made with two round or two square ends. Work the buttonhole stitching using ordinary sewing thread.

1. Mark the centre and length of the button-hole with a line. Stitch a small rectangle of running- or machine-stitch 3 mm ($\frac{1}{8}$ in) away around the line to mark the outside of the stitching. Carefully cut the buttonhole (**K**).

2. Secure a thread at the lower left-hand corner at the square end of the buttonhole. Bring the needle through from back to front just outside the stitched line and pass it under the point of the needle from left to right (**L**). Pull the needle through and draw the thread upwards so the knot that has formed sits on the fabric edge. Work stitches in this way close together along to the round end of the buttonhole.

3. At the round end, work seven stitches radiating around the end. Turn the work and stitch back along the other straight edge (**M**). On the last stitch, pass the needle through the knot of the first stitch and out at the base of the last stitch to pull the two edges together. Stitch two long stitches across the length of the square end, then turn the work and stitch the square end with the knots of the stitches towards the buttonhole.

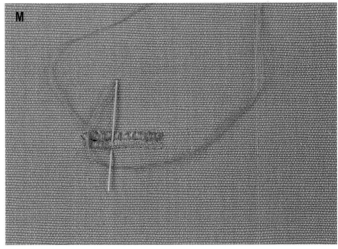

HOOKS AND EYES

Hooks and eyes are used to fasten two butting edges. Use double thread for strength and position the hook towards the edge with its end 3 mm ($\frac{1}{8}$ in) in from the edge.

Stitch around over each hole on the hook without stitching through to the right side, then stitch two or three stitches over the neck of the hook to secure it. Position the eye to match so it projects 3 mm ($\frac{1}{8}$ in) over the fabric edge. Stitch around each hole, then over each side edge of the eye (**N**).

HOOKS AND BARS

Hooks and bars, or straight eyes, are used to fasten two overlapping edges, such as on a waistband. For a bar or straight eye, mark its position with a pin to match the hook. Stitch around the first hole of the bar, then slip the needle between the fabric layers to the other hole and stitch around that. Two hooks and bars are often stitched side by side to fasten a waistband (**O**).

PRESS STUDS

Press stud fasteners are used to make a small, fairly lightweight fastening. They are available in a good range of sizes, and in silver, black or clear plastic. One half of the fastener has a ball, and the other a socket which clips the two halves together.

Using double thread, stitch the ball half of the stud to the overlapping edge with three or four stitches through each of the holes around the stud. Close the opening and pass a pin through the hole at the centre of the stud to mark the position for the other half, then stitch the socket half in place in the same way as before (**P**).

N

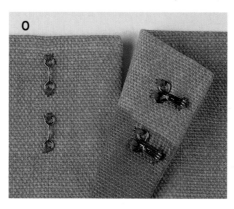

O

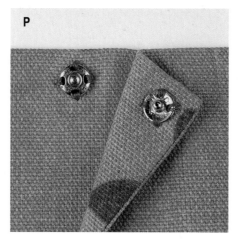

P

Non-sew stud fastenings

Available in a range of styles and sizes, non-sew studs can make fairly sturdy fastenings. They are usually hammered or snapped in place with tools provided with the kit, or purchased separately. These fasteners usually have a decorative cap, and the top layer of fabric is held between this and the socket. The ball half is then attached to the other fabric layer with a rivet on the wrong side.

VELCRO™

Sometimes called touch and close fastener, Velcro™ has two halves: one is covered in tiny soft loops, and the other is covered with minute hooks that fasten onto the loops firmly when the halves are pushed together (**Q**). Velcro™ is available in strip form for fastening long edges, and also in small, round spots for joining overlapping edges. Velcro™ is also available with one sewable side and one adhesive side, which is useful for attaching fabric or blinds to a frame.

Stitch Velcro™ in place along the flat areas at the edge by machine or by hand, hemstitching over the edge.

Q

Buttoned Cushion

This cushion has two panels at the front. Each panel is finished with a deep hem that overlaps and fastens together with buttons. This design creates a useful opening for the cushion pad as well as a decorative feature.

MATERIALS

1 m (40 in) furnishing fabric
Sewing thread
Three 2 cm ($\frac{3}{4}$ in) buttons
Cushion pad, 40 cm (15 $\frac{3}{4}$ in) square

CUTTING OUT

1 Cut two pieces of fabric for the front of the cushion, one 36.5 cm x 43 cm (14$\frac{3}{8}$ x 17 in) and one 22 x 43 cm (8$\frac{3}{4}$ x 17 in). Cut a piece for the back as well that is 43 cm (17 in) squared. This measurement includes 1.5 cm ($\frac{5}{8}$ in) seam allowances.

STITCHING

1 Press 1 cm ($\frac{3}{8}$ in) then 4.5 cm (1$\frac{3}{4}$ in) hems to the wrong side along one 43 cm (17 in) long edge on each front piece. Machine-stitch in place.

2 Mark three buttonhole positions on the hem of the narrower front piece, one at the centre, then two others 10 cm (4 in) on either side. Mark the buttonholes at right angles to the hem edge and beginning 1.5 cm ($\frac{5}{8}$ in) in from the hem edge, making sure they are long enough to fit the buttons. Stitch and then cut the buttonholes.

3 Overlap the two hems with right sides uppermost and the buttonhole hem on top. Mark the buttons' positions on the under-hem and stitch them in place (**diagram 1**).

DIAGRAM 1

4 Fasten the buttons. Place the back piece of the cushion to the front with right sides facing and raw edges level and stitch together around the outer edges, leaving a 1.5 cm ($^5/_8$ in) seam all around. Trim the corners and press the seams open as far as possible. Unfasten the buttons, turn the cover right-side out and press the seam at the edge.

Moving buttons

Unpick the button, then place the buttonhole over to where the new fastening is required. Pin through the end of the buttonhole to mark the new button position. Carefully pull away the buttonhole leaving the pin in place. Stitch the button onto the new marked position, remembering to make a thread shank if required (see page 56).

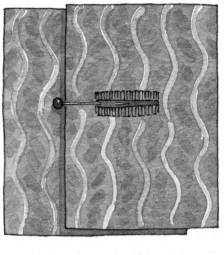

TORN BUTTONS
Buttons can get pulled off, taking a piece of fabric with them. The fabric will need to be repaired before the button can be restitched. To do this, cut a circle of mending tape a little smaller than the button. Iron it to the wrong side of the button position. On the right side, work rows of machine-stitch or hand running stitch backwards and forwards across the circle to reinforce the area. Re-stitch the button in place.

Zip Bags

Neat zip bags can serve a number of purposes. Here we show you how to make a zip bag that can easily be used to hold cosmetics or toiletries. Iron-on interfacing is added to give extra body to the fabric. For a durable, wipe-clean finish, you can also add optional lining made from shower curtain lining fabric.

MATERIALS

½ m (20 in) cotton furnishing fabric
½ m (20 in) iron-on interfacing
20 cm (8 in) zip
Sewing thread
Shower curtain lining fabric (optional)

CUTTING OUT

1 To make a small cosmetics bag, cut two pieces of cotton furnishing fabric to 24 x 18 cm (9½ x 7 in). Cut two pieces the same size from the interfacing. Seam allowances measuring 1.5 cm (⅝ in) are included.

Large toiletry bag

Larger bags can be made in this way as well. To make the toiletry bag shown on page 65, you will need two pieces of cotton furnishing fabric measuring 34 x 28 cm (13½ x 11 in), the same amount of interfacing, and a 30 cm (12 in) zip. Make in the same way as the cosmetics bag.

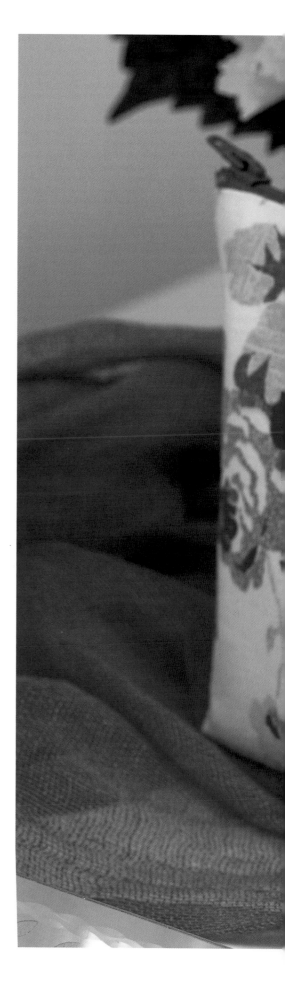

STITCHING

1 Apply the interfacing to the wrong side of the fabric panels. Stitch the zip to the centre of the two long top edges using the exposed zip method (see page 55).

2 With right sides facing, raw edges level and the zip partway open, stitch the two bag pieces together around the side and base edges. Press the seams open (**diagram 1**).

DIAGRAM 1

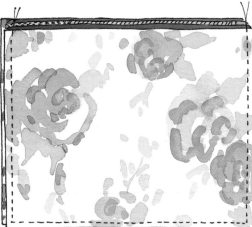

3 Separate two layers at the lower corners and refold them diagonally, so that the side and base seams are on top of each other at the centre of the point. Stitch across at right

angles to the seams 4.5 cm ($1\frac{3}{4}$ in) in from the points (**diagram 2**). Trim the point away 1 cm ($\frac{3}{8}$ in) above the stitching. Turn the bag right-side out.

DIAGRAM 2

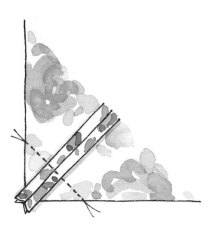

4 To make an optional lining, cut two pieces of lining fabric to the same size as the bag. Sew the lining bag together as you did the outer fabric bag. Place the lining inside the bag, right side facing out. Tuck it under the raw edge of the lining around the top edge, level with the zip stitching. Hand-stitch the lining to the back of the zip stitching.

Replacing a zip

When replacing a zip, the first thing to do is to note the way the original zip was stitched, so that the replacement zip can be stitched in the same way. First, unpick the zip as far as possible. While unpicking, you may encounter difficulty where the ends of the zip tape are stitched inside the waistband or collar. Often the best solution to this problem is to snip through the zip tape, leaving the ends inside the waistband, then pin and tack the new zip in place.

Sometimes it is possible to unpick a few stitches at the waistband and to tuck the ends of the zip tape in before restitching. If this is not possible, however, fold the ends of the zip tape back at an angle, as shown, then stitch the zip in place and handstitch the folded back tape.

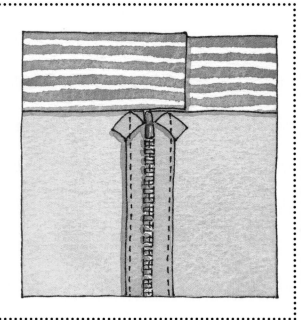

Piping, Gathers and Pleats

There are many ways to apply decorative finishes to sewn items –

piping, gathers and pleats all add interest in different ways.

PIPING

Piping can be bought ready-made with a projecting flange to insert in a seam, or it can be made by covering piping cord with a strip of bias-cut fabric to match your item. Covering piping with checked and striped fabrics can be especially effective.

Cutting bias strips

Fold the fabric diagonally so the cross-grain is level with, or parallel to the selvedges (see page 12). Cut along the diagonal fold, and then cut the bias strips along the cut edge, making them wide enough to cover the cord plus two 1.5 cm ($\frac{5}{8}$ in) seam allowances.

Joining the strips

1. If a long bias strip is required, trim the two ends on the straight grain. Place the two ends together with right sides facing, the straight ends level and the fold lines intersecting 6 mm ($\frac{1}{4}$ in) in. Pin to hold.

2. Stitch the two ends together, taking a 6 mm ($\frac{1}{4}$ in) seam (**A**). Press the seam open. Trim the seam corners level with the edge.

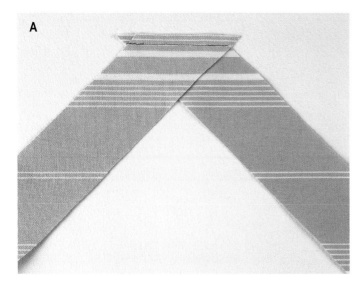

A

Covering piping cord

Place the cord at the centre of the bias strip and wrap the strip around the cord so that the raw edges of the strip are level. Using the zipper foot on your sewing machine, stitch along the flat area (flange) close to the cord, but not right next to it (**B**).

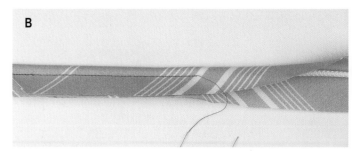

B

Joining ends

1. Stitch the piping in place to the right side of the fabric, keeping the raw edges level and stitching along the line of the previous stitching. Leave about 2.5 cm (1 in) unstitched at each end of the piping.

2. Cut the piping so it overlaps the first end by 2.5 cm (1 in). Unpick the end of the piping to reveal the cord and snip away the cord level with the facing cord.

3. Fold the raw edges under on the overlapping end and lap it over the beginning. Complete the stitching (**C**).

C

Finishing ends

At the end of a strip of piping, snip away the cord only at the finishing point, leaving some of the bias strip fabric intact. Fold the end of the bias strip diagonally across into the seam allowance and stitch into place (**D**).

D

Curves and corners

When you are attaching piping that goes around corners, you will need to snip into the flat area 1.5 cm ($\frac{5}{8}$ in) in from the corner, so it will open out to fit around the corner with the raw edges level with the next edge (**E**). On most curved seams the bias cut strip has enough give to fit around without the need to snip, but if it does not, snip at intervals.

E

Using ready-made piping

There are two types of ready-made piping: one has an inner cord covered by fabric, which can be stitched in the same way as piping you have made yourself. The other type has no inner cord, just a cord woven onto an attached flat area.

When joining ends of the latter type, it is best to overlap the ends diagonally into the seam allowance (**F**). Leave the piping unstitched for a little way on each side of the join. Press the overlapping ends as flat as they'll go, or if possible, unravel the ends of the piping to flatten it where it goes into the seam. Overlap the ends diagonally into the seam allowance and complete the stitching.

F

GATHERS

Gathers, which take in fullness, are often used to form a frill, a skirt, or a curtain. Less formal gathers are usually formed along the entire edge, while more tailored pleats can be repeated, spaced at intervals or made at corners. For gathers, allow one and a half times the required finished length of fabric.

Stitching a gather

Gathered stitching can be done by hand using running stitch, or by machine. Using a machine is quicker and will produce more even gathers. A single row of gathering stitches can be worked along the seamline, but a double row will allow the fabric to hang more neatly.

1. Adjust the machine stitch to its longest length and stitch along 1.5 cm ($\frac{5}{8}$ in) from the edge, leaving the threads ends. Stitch a second row of gathering 6 mm ($\frac{1}{4}$ in) above the first row. On long frills, stop and restart the stitching to divide the gathered edge up into about 75 cm (30 in) lengths (**G**).

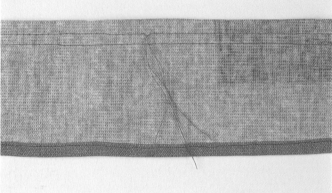

Attaching a gather frill

1. Divide the frill and the edge it is to be stitched to into an equal number of sections and mark with pins. Pin the two edges together with right sides facing at the marker pins. Pull both the gathering threads on the wrong side of the frill together while sliding the fabric along to form a gathered frill (**H**).

2. When the gathers fit, wind the thread ends around a pin in a figure of eight to hold. Adjust the gathers evenly, then pin, tack and stitch in place just below the seamline (**I**).

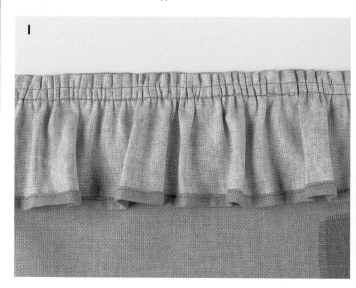

PLEATS

Pleats can be pressed to give a sharp crease down the length of the pleat, or they can be left unpressed so that the pleats are held at the top edge only for a less formal look. To make pleats, allow twice as much fabric as the required finished width.

Knife pleats

These are a series of single pleats facing in the same direction, usually towards the right.

1. Measure and mark the depth of the required pleats at the top edge, and at intervals down the length using pins or an erasable marker pen.

2. Fold one marking over to meet the other to form the pleats. Press the pleats, removing the pins as you reach them. Pin, then tack along the seamline at the top edge. If making rows of pleats, machine-stitch across the top edge to hold them in place (**J**).

Box pleats

Box pleats are formed by creating two pleats facing away from each other (**K**). Measure and mark the depth of the pleats required at the top edge and at intervals down the length with pins or an erasable marker pen. Fold the two inner markings outwards, away from each other to meet the outer markings. Press the pleats, removing the pins as you reach them. Pin, then tack along the seamline at the top edge. If making rows of pleats, machine-stitch across the top edge to hold the pleats in place.

Inverted pleats

These are formed from two pleats facing towards each other so that the two folds meet at the centre.

1. Measure and mark the depth of the required pleats at the top edge and at intervals down the length with pins or an erasable marker pen.

2. Fold the two outer markings inwards towards each other to meet at the centre marking. Press the pleats, removing the pins as you reach them. Pin, then tack along the seam line at the top edge (**L**). If making rows of pleats, machine-stitch across the top edge to hold the pleats in place.

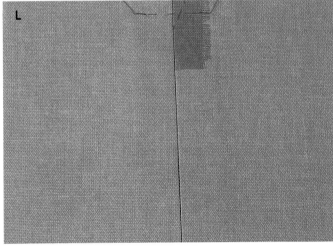

Chair Seat Cover

Smartly striped in cool, neutral shades, this elegant seat cover will add charm to a simple dining chair. The pleated skirt cover follows the stripes to make the pleats, and is finished at the top with a neat piping in the seam.

MATERIALS

Pattern paper
Pencil
1 m (40 in) furnishing fabric
1.5 m (60 in) piping cord
Sewing thread

CUTTING OUT

1 Lay the pattern paper on the chair seat and draw the seat outline. Add on 1.5 cm ($^5/_8$ in) to the side and front edges and 3 cm ($1^1/_4$ in) to the back edge for seam allowances. Cut out.

2 Measure around the side and front edge of the seat pattern and cut the skirt approximately twice that length, allowing extra for joins by 23 cm (9 in).

3 Cut a strip of extra fabric on the bias to cover the piping. You will need to measure around the seat for the amount required. Cut fabric for four ties, each 4 x 40 cm ($1^1/_2$ x 15 $^3/_4$ in).

STITCHING

1 Cover the piping cord with the bias strip. Stitch the piping around the chair seat, finishing the ends of the piping 3 cm ($1^1/_4$ in) in from the back edge.

2 Press a 1 cm ($^3/_8$ in) then a 2.5 cm (1 in) hem to the wrong side along the lower edge of the skirt.

3 Form and press the skirt pleats, if possible using the fabric stripes as a guide. For the pleats shown here, 4 cm ($1^1/_2$ in) is taken out in each pleat, and the crease of each pleat is 4 cm ($1^1/_2$ in) from the following one (**diagram 1**). Allow at least 6 cm ($2^1/_4$ in) of fabric to be free from pleats at each end.

DIAGRAM 1

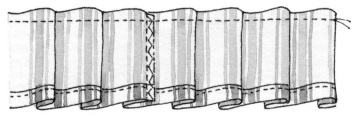

4 Join the skirt pieces at the inside fold of the pleat by stitching the seam through both fabric and hem. Press the pleats at the complete length required, then pin, tack and machine-stitch the pleats in place 1.5 cm ($^5/_8$ in) down from the top edge.

DIAGRAM 2

5 Pin the skirt in place around the seat with right sides facing and the raw edges and the back edges level. Stitch in place along the line of, or just inside, the piping stitching (**diagram 2**).

6 Press 1 cm ($^3/_8$ in) then 2 cm ($^3/_8$ in) to the wrong side along the back edges of the skirt and seat. Machine-stitch in place, stopping and restarting the stitching at the piped seam.

7 To make the ties, press 1 cm ($^3/_8$ in) to the wrong side along the two long edges and one short edge of each tie piece. Press each in half so the raw edges are enclosed and machine-stitch down the long edge. Place the cover on the chair and pin the ends of the ties in position under the hem at the top of the skirt and on the back edge to fasten around the back uprights. Remove the chair cover and stitch the ties in place.

Pretty Paisley Chair Seat Cover Variation

This pretty variation of the chair seat cover has a gathered skirt, contrast piping and cut-out back corners to accommodate the chair back's uprights. Paisley print fabric is teamed with plain 2.5 cm (1 in) bias binding to finish the cut-out back corners and to cover the piping cord.

Cut out the fabric, allowing one and a half times the finished length for the gathered skirt. Bind the corners with the bias binding, making little mitred pleats at the inner corners. Open out the remaining bias binding, press it flat, and use it to cover the piping cord. Make up the cover, gathering the skirt to fit around the side and front edges.

Finishing Touches

Decorative touches will add designer details to simple projects in a surprisingly quick and easy way. An appliqué motif personalizes an item, elegant bows add a bold impact and a hand-stitched fringe adds a discrete but stylish detail.

BOWS

1. Cut a strip of fabric twice the required width plus 2 cm (¾ in). Fold the strip in half lengthways and tie into a bow to establish the required length, allowing an extra 2 cm (¾ in) for seams. Untie the bow. Fold the strip in half lengthways with right sides facing and raw edges level. Stitch along the two short edges and the long edge 1 cm (⅜ in) in from the edge, leaving an opening at the centre of the long edge for an opening (**A**).

A

2. Trim the corners and turn the strip right-side out. Press the seams at the edge, stitch the opening closed and tie into a bow (**B**).

B

TIES

Cut the ties to the required finished length plus 2 cm (¾ in), and twice the width plus 2 cm (¾ in). Press 1 cm (⅜ in) to the wrong side across one short end (or both if they show) and the two long edges. Press the tie in half lengthways. Tack, then stitch down the long edge and across the pressed end (**C**).

C

APPLYING LACE AND BRAID

Lace and braids can be stitched to the surface of fabric or to the edge by hand or machine. If you are attaching braid to the surface of the fabric, pin and tack the braid in place, then stitch in place by hand with running stitch, backstitch or small hem stitches over the edge. Alternatively, machine-stitch with straight or zigzag stitches. When applying lace or braid to a fabric edge, a neat finish is obtained when the raw edge is folded to the wrong side first so the zigzag stitching attaches the lace and neatens the fabric edge at the same time (**D**).

D

STITCHING CORD

Cords give a finished look when they are stitched to the edge of items such as cushions. Hold the cord in place with one hand and stitch with the other, taking a small straight stitch through the underside of the cord, then a longer diagonal stitch through the fabric from one side to the other (**E**).

E

HEMSTITCHED FRINGE

This type of hemstitching is a form of counted thread work and is different from ordinary hemstitching. It is best worked on an even-weave fabric so the threads can be counted.

1. Pull out a few threads along where the fringe's top will be. Working right to left along the top edge of the fringe, bring the needle out a few threads in from the drawn threads.

2. Take the needle up to the pulled thread and pass it through behind a bunch of four threads. Pull through, reinsert the needle at the start of the four threads and bring it out level with the end of the bunch. Repeat (**F**).

3. When the hemstitching is complete, pull the threads away to form the fringe.

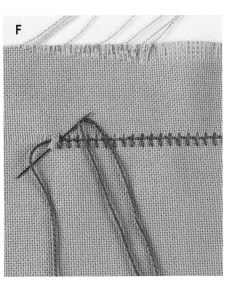

EMBROIDERY STITCHES
Blanket stitch

This stitch is often worked at the edge of a fabric to give a decorative finish. It can also be worked at the edges of appliqué shapes.

1. Working from left to right, bring the needle out at the lower edge of the stitch, insert it at the top of the stitch and bring it out at the bottom with the thread under the needlepoint.

2. Pull the needle through to form a loop. Move the needle along to the right and repeat (**G**).

Chain stitch

1. Working so the stitches are coming towards you, bring the needle out at the top of the line and hold the thread down with your left thumb.

2. Insert the needle where it last came out and bring the point out a short distance away, then pull the needle through, keeping the thread under the needle to form the loop.

Insert the needle where it last came out and continue. Single chain stitches can be worked to make a daisy stitch by taking a small stitch over the end of the formed loop (**H**).

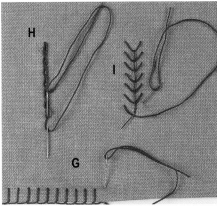

Fly stitch

Bring the needle through at the top left, holding it down with your left thumb. Insert the needle across to the right at the same level and bring it out diagonally downwards centrally between the top two stitches. Take a straight stitch downwards and repeat (**I**).

APPLIQUÉ

Appliqué is the application of cut-out fabric shapes to other pieces of fabric to make a design or pattern. The process is made wonderfully easy by the use of a special backing fabric called "fusible web", which fuses onto the fabric shape to be appliquéd. This prevents the edges from fraying and does away with the need to tack.

Making an appliqué shape

Draw out or trace your chosen design onto paper, then trace it onto the paper side of the fusible web. (If you are using fusible web, the design will be reversed, so if the design has an obvious left or right, you will need to draw the design in reverse). Cut out the shapes roughly and apply the fusible web to the wrong side of the appliqué fabric. Cut out the pieces, then peel off the paper backing (**J**). Arrange the appliqué pieces onto your fabric and iron them in place following the manufacturer's instructions.

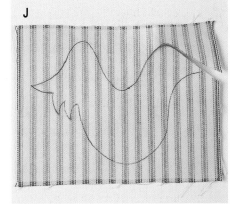

Edging an appliqué shape

With fusible web you don't need to stitch around the pieces if you prefer not too, but doing so can add definition. Stitch around the edge with a simple running stitch just inside the edge (**K**). Alternatively, you can work a blanket stitch around the edge.

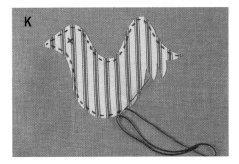

Zigzag stitching appliqué

Zigzag stitching is another decorative option. Adjust the machine to a medium-width, close zigzag stitch and stitch around the appliquéd shapes. When stitching curves, stop every few stitches with the needle down on the outer edge of the curve, raise the presser foot and turn the fabric slightly to realign the edge. On inner curves, stop with the needle down on the inner curve. Tie off all thread ends on the wrong side to finish (**L**).

Pockets and Patches

Pockets make handy storage spaces. They can be added to many sewn items, including clothing, bags, chair arm covers and wall tidies. A pocket can also act as a patch when it is used to cover a repaired tear or hole. Traditional patches are used to repair torn garments. If you cannot find a good fabric match to make a concealed repair, consider a contrasting or patterned fabric to add a decorative feature.

POCKETS

There are two types of simple pockets that can be added to sewn items: one is a patch pocket and the other is a pocket with gussets. A patch pocket is a flat piece of fabric stitched in place around three sides. It is commonly used on clothes and on the outside and inside of bags. A pocket with gussets has a concealed pleat of extra fabric down both sides of the pocket to provide more space inside the pockets. This type of pocket is usually used on wall hangings and tidies, where larger items may be stored.

Patch pockets

Patch pockets are usually made from rectangles or squares of fabric.

1. Decide on the required finished size and add a 1.5 cm (⅝ in) seam allowance to the side and lower edges and a hem allowance of 3 cm (1¼ in) at the top. Press the seam allowance to the wrong side around the side and lower edges. At the top edge, press 1 cm (⅜ in), then another 2 cm (¾ in) to the wrong side (**A**). Alternatively, on thicker fabric, zigzag stitch the top edge and fold down a single hem.

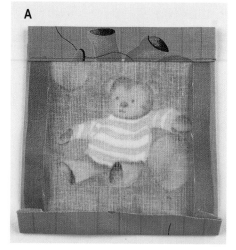

A

2. Place the pocket in the required position and pin in place. The pins are best placed at right angles to the edges and diagonally into the lower corners.

3. To sew the pocket onto the garment, start with reverse stitching at one top corner, then continue to stitch down one side, across the base and back up the other side (**B**). Finish with reverse stitching to secure the pocket.

B

Pockets with gussets

1. Decide on the pocket size in the same way as for the patch pocket (see left), then add on a gusset allowance, for example 4 cm (1½ in), to each side edge. This may make the cut piece of fabric wider than it is tall even though the finished pocket will be taller than it is wide. Make the pocket in the same way as the patch pocket.

2. Press 4 cm (1½ in) to the wrong side down the side edge, then press the edge back level with the fold to make a 2 cm (¾ in)-wide pleat under each side edge (**C**).

C

3. Place the pocket in position, lift the gusset fold carefully, and pin the side edges in place. Open the gusset out, and tack and stitch the side edges only.

4. Refold the gussets and stitch across the bottom of the pocket through all layers. Remember to start and finish with reverse stitching (**D**).

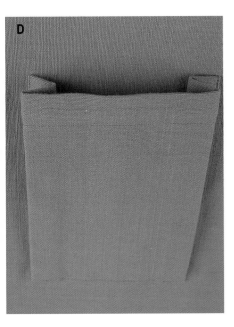

D

Divided pockets

A divided pocket can add an individual touch to a plain patch pocket; the divided section looks attractive and can be made to fit items such as small pens and notebooks, lipsticks, a toothbrush, or cutlery in a cutlery roll.

1. Decide on the required finished size for the entire pocket and add seams and hems as for the patch pocket (see opposite). Cut out and stitch the pocket on the garment in the same way as the patch pocket (see opposite).

2. Mark and pin the sections you want to divide and check that your items will fit snugly. Stitch the sections from the top to bottom either by following the line of the pins, removing them as you reach them, or by drawing a line with an erasable marker to stitch along (**E**).

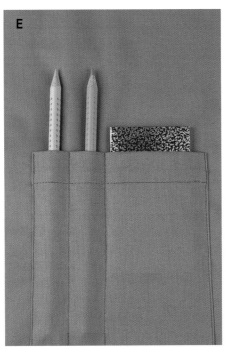

E

Mending a torn pocket

A torn top corner is one of the most common pocket repairs needed, particularly on utility items such as overalls or aprons, where the pockets can get caught on handles or hooks. Sometimes the stitching just gives, but more often the fabric behind the pocket tears.

1. First reinforce the tear area with a square of fabric, iron-on mending tape, or lightweight iron-on interfacing. You will need to cut a piece about 1 cm (⅜ in) larger than the size of the tear. Tack or iron-on the reinforcing fabric to the wrong side of the tear, ensuring that the edges meet neatly.

2. Using a matching thread, stitch along the tear with a three-step zigzag or with small running stitches worked backwards and forwards across the tear in a tight zigzag formation (**F**).

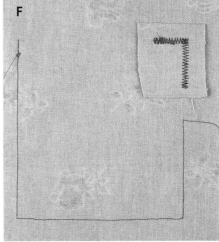

F

3. Trim away any excess fabric on the wrong side and restitch the pocket (**G**).

G

PATCHES

Patches are typically used to mend or cover tears, holes and worn areas, but sometimes they are added to a garment solely as a decorative feature.

Handstitched patch

This method works well for light-to-medium-weight fabric tears and holes. If you can match the fabric pattern, the patch can be almost invisible. Larger repairs, such as on sheets, can be machine-stitched for greater ease if preferred.

1. Trim the worn or torn area to a square or rectangle. Snip a short, diagonal cut into each corner and press the raw edges to the wrong side around the hole (**H**).

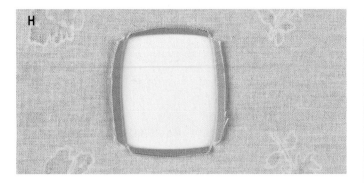

2. Cut a patch 2 – 2.5 cm (¾ – 1 in) larger than the hole and press the raw edge to the right side around its edges (**I**).

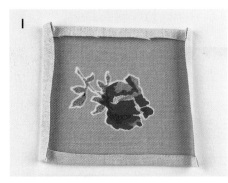

3. Place the patch to wrong side of the hole. Handstitch in place around the outer edge of the patch, taking small stitches through the main fabric. Turn to the right side and hand-stitch around the hole to the patch, this time making small stitches on the right side (**J**).

Zigzag-stitched patch

This robust method is suited to thick fabrics such as heavyweight denim, where the hand-stitched method would be too bulky. The patch will be functional, but not invisible.

1. Trim the tear or worn area to a neat oval shape (**K**). Cut the trimmed hole size from the centre of a piece of fusible web.

2. Apply the fusible web to the wrong side of the patch fabric following the manufacturer's instructions. Cut out a patch 2 cm (¾ in) larger than the hole (**L**).

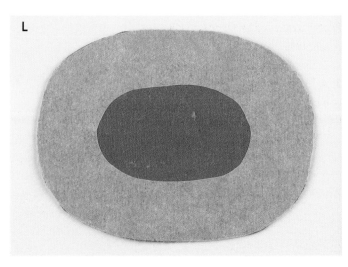

3. Steam press to fuse the patch in place. Zigzag stitch around the outer edge of the patch with a wide, close stitch (**M**). If fusible web is not available, the same method can still be used, but you will need to zigzag stitch around the hole as well.

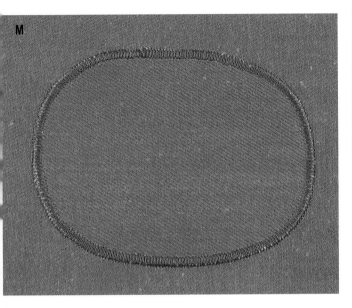

Mending a trouser pocket

Trouser pockets – or any pocket hanging inside a garment – can become worn, but can be easily fixed for a new lease on life.

1. Cut away the worn area and use it as a pattern. Cut a double layer of fabric using the pattern, adding on 2 cm ($\frac{3}{8}$ in) to the straight cut edges for seams.

2. Unpick the pocket seams a little way past the cut edges. Stitch the new pieces to the cut edges, taking 1 cm ($\frac{3}{8}$ in) for seams. Zigzag stitch the edges together and press downwards.

3. Restitch the seam around the outer edge of the pocket and zigzag stitch the edges together (**N**).

Decorative patch

Sometimes, especially on children's clothes, it is possible to turn a repair into a decorative patch that is a feature as well as functional. An irregular shape and uneven stitching will add to the naïve charm. If the item is to be laundered frequently, the edge can be zigzag stitched before handstitching.

1. Apply fusible web to the wrong side of the patch fabric following the manufacturer's instructions. Cut out the patch to the required size and steam press to fuse the patch in place.

2. Handstitch large, uneven crossed stitches over the edges using a contrast embroidery thread (**O**).

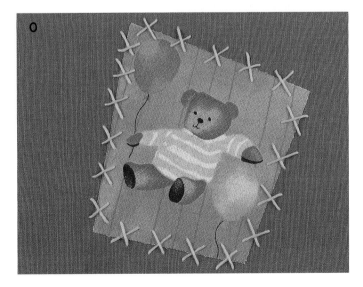

Calico Shopping Bag

This simple shopping bag is decorated with pretty appliqué daisies. You can use this method to add any design you like to a similar item.

MATERIALS
Pattern paper
1 m (40 in) calico fabric
1 m (40 in) firm iron-on interfacing
1 m (40 in) lining fabric
$\frac{1}{2}$ m (20 in) fusible web
Fabric oddments for appliqué
Sewing threads to match calico and appliqué fabrics

CUTTING OUT
1 Cut out a paper pattern 47 cm ($18\frac{1}{2}$ in) wide by 36 cm ($14\frac{1}{4}$ in) deep (this includes 1.5 cm ($\frac{5}{8}$ in) seam allowances). Using the pattern, cut two pieces each from the calico, interfacing and lining. Cut two handles 9 cm ($3\frac{1}{2}$ in) x 60 cm ($23\frac{1}{2}$ in) from the calico.

2 Mark an area on your paper pattern 6 cm ($2\frac{1}{4}$ in) in from the side and base edges and 1.5 cm ($\frac{5}{8}$ in) down from the top edge of your front piece. Trace the flower design from page 92 and transfer it to the pattern (**diagram 1**), keeping within the marked area. You may need to scale the design up or down to fit.

STITCHING
1 Apply the iron-on interfacing to the wrong side of the calico pieces. Lightly mark the positions for the flower stems on the front area on one calico piece. Adjust the machine to a wide, close zigzag stitch and stitch the stems in satin stitch. Pull the thread end through to the wrong side and knot together to finish. Cut out and apply the appliqué design, stitching around the edges with a zigzag stitch.

2 Stitch the two calico pieces facing together around the side and base edges. Stitch the linings together in the same way, but leave a 15 cm (6 in) gap on the base edge. Press the seams open.

3 Open out the lower corners and refold them diagonally so the side and base seams are on top of the other at the centre of the point. Stitch across at right angles to the seams 4.5 cm ($1\frac{1}{2}$ in) in from the point in the same way as for the zip bag (see page 62). Trim the point away above the stitching. Stitch the lining corners in the same way.

DIAGRAM 1

4 Press 1.5 cm ($^{5}/_{8}$ in) to the wrong side along both long edges of the handles. Press the handles in half lengthways and stitch along both long edges. With the handles pointing downwards, pin and tack their ends to the top edge of the bag 11 cm ($4^{1}/_{4}$ in) in from the side seams (**diagram 2**).

DIAGRAM 2

5 Place the lining to the bag with right sides facing and the top edges level so the handles are sandwiched, and stitch the lining to the bag around the top edge. Turn the bag right side out through the gap in the lining stitching. Handstitch the gap in the lining closed. Press the lining to the inside of the bag and topstitch around the top edge to finish.

MAKING A FIRM BASE

A fabric-covered cardboard insert will give the bag a firm base and help it keep its shape. First, cut the cardboard to the size of the base of the bag, then cut a piece of lining fabric twice as wide as the card, plus seam allowances all round. Fold the fabric in half lengthways and stitch together along one short and one long edge. Turn the fabric right-side out and press. Slip the cardboard into the fabric sleeve, tuck in the remaining raw edges and handstitch them together.

Wall Hanging with Pockets

Pockets of bold, bright colours add a modern feel to this useful wall tidy. The spacious pockets have folded side gussets for extra space, making it a great hold-all for toys, accessories, shoes – even your sewing kit! We used a different colour oddment of fabric for each pocket, but this wall hanging would look just as good using the same colour fabric for all of the pockets.

MATERIALS

1.5 m (60 in) calico fabric
(for background of hanging)
9 assorted cotton fabric oddments,
each at least 23 x 21 cm (9 x 8 ¼ in)
1 m (40 in) medium-weight interlining
Sewing thread

CUTTING OUT

1 Cut two pieces of calico and one from the interlining, each 48 x 68 cm (19 x 26¾ in) (1.5 cm (⅝ in) seam allowances are included). Cut a calico strip 12 x 80 cm (4¾ x 31½ in) for the tabs. Cut nine pockets from the fabric oddments, each 23 x 21 cm (9 x 8¼ in).

STITCHING

1 Press 1.5 cm (⅝ in) to the wrong side down the two shorter side edges and the lower edge of the first pocket. Press a 1 cm (⅜ in), then a 2 cm (¾ in) hem to the wrong side along the top edge and stitch in place. On each side edge, press 4 cm (1½ in) to wrong side, then 2 cm (¾ in) back to the right side to form a gusset (**diagram 1**). Make up all nine pockets in this way.

DIAGRAM 1

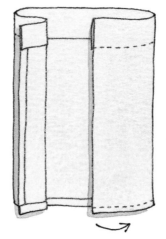

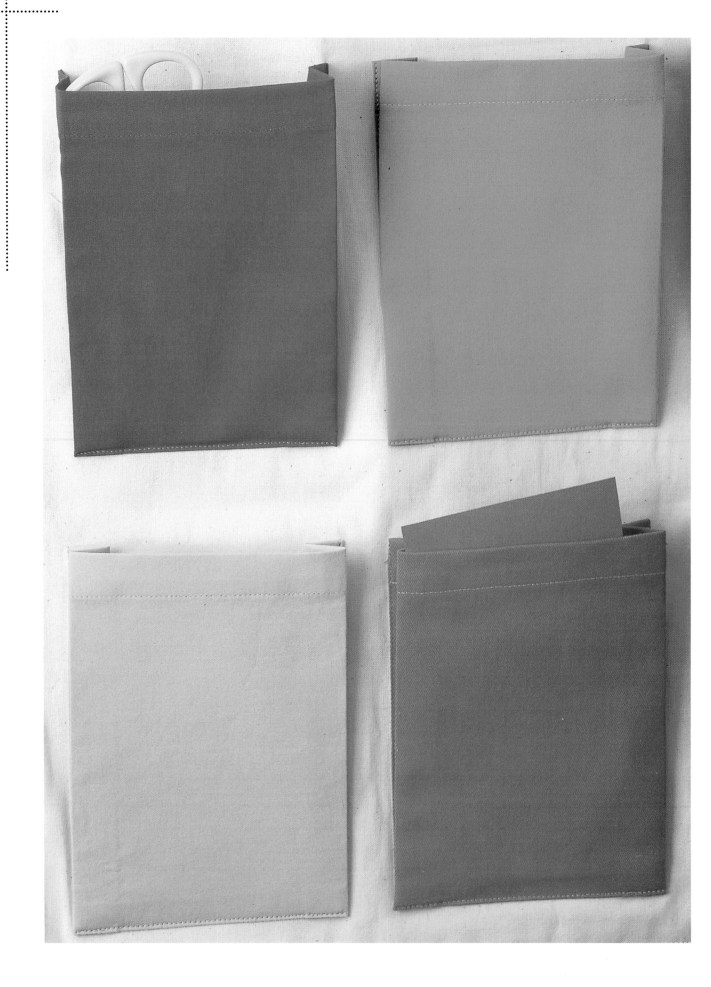

2 Arrange the pockets with the gussets folded in on one main piece of the backing fabric with the top edges of the top pockets about 6.5 cm (2½ in) down. Place the sides of the pockets about 2 cm (¾ in) apart and allow 4 cm (1½ in) between the rows and at the side and bottom edges.

3 Pin the side edges of the pockets in place carefully, lifting up the gusset to do so. Stitch the two side edges of each pocket. Refold the gussets and stitch across the bottom edges with the gussets folded.

4 Fold the tab strip in half lengthways and stitch along the length. Trim the seam, turn the tab right side out and press the seam at one edge. Topstitch along the two long sides, near the edges.

5 Cut the tab strip into four equal lengths and fold each tab in half. Pin and tack the tabs in position, making sure that they are 2.5 cm (1 in) in from the side edges, and evenly spaced. The tabs should point downwards and the raw edges should be level (**diagram 2**).

6 Place the interlining to the wrong side of the backing piece, then place the remaining calico piece to the right side of the backing. Stitch together through all layers leaving a 20 cm (8 in) gap at the lower edge to turn through. Trim the interlining from the seam allowance and trim the seam allowance and corners.

7 Turn the wall hanging right-side out and press the seam to the edge. Tuck in the seam allowances along the opening and handsitch the edges together. Topstitch around the outer edge of the wall hanging to finish if you like.

DIAGRAM 2

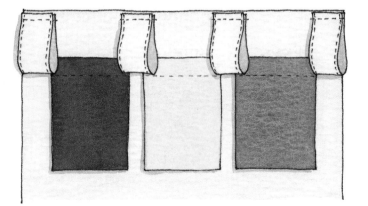

Cutlery Roll

Add a refined touch to *al fresco* dining with an individual cutlery roll that keeps the cutlery in a divided pocket and unrolls to form a placemat. Here, a toile de jouy fabric design with idyllic rural scenes perfectly echoes this outdoor theme.

MATERIALS

1 m (40 in) cotton toile de jouy fabric
½ m (20 in) medium-weight interlining
Sewing thread
1 m (40 in) ribbon

CUTTING OUT

1 Cut out two fabric pieces and one interlining piece, each 44 x 30 cm (17¼ x12 in) (1.5 cm (⅝ in) seam allowances are included), and a pocket 12 x 18 cm (4¾ x 7 in).

2 Cut a 4.5 cm (1¾ in)-wide bias strip long enough to fit around the outer edge of the finished roll, joining if required.

STITCHING

1 Sandwich the interlining between the two fabric pieces with the fabric right side outside, and pin together. Using a small cup or jar as a template, draw around at the corners to make curved corners. Trim away the excess fabric. Stitch together through all layers around the edge about 6 mm (¼ in) in from the edge.

2 Press 1.5 cm (⅝ in) to the wrong side down the side edges of the pocket. Press 1 cm (⅜ in), then a 2 cm (¾ in) hem to the wrong side across the top edge of the pocket and stitch in place.

3 Place the pocket on the mat with its side edge 3 cm (1¼ in) from the side edge of the mat and its lower raw edge level with edge of the mat. Stitch in place down both side edges.

4 Stitch two more rows down the pocket, each 3 cm (1¼ in) from the sides, to divide the pocket into three 3 cm (1¼ in)-wide sections.

5 Fold the ribbon in half and tack the fold. On the opposite side edge to the pocket, tack the ribbon level with the edge of the mat at the centre and on the other side of the mat (**diagram 1**).

DIAGRAM 1

6 Press the long edges of the crossway strip towards the centre of the strip so they nearly meet at the centre, then press the strip in half so the under-half is just slightly wider than the top half.

7 Arranging so the join will be on a straight edge, insert the edge of the mat inside the binding with the narrower half uppermost. Pin the binding in place, gently easing it, and steam press it to shape around the corners (**diagram 2**). Join the ends with a diagonal seam or by the overlapping method (see page 35). Machine-stitch the binding in place through all layers so that the fold of the ribbon is caught in the stitching.

DIAGRAM 2

Calico Shopping Bag Template (see page 80)

Suppliers

UK

Coats Crafts UK
PO Box 22
Lingfield Point,
McMullen Road
Darlington,
Co Durham, DL1 1YQ
Tel (01325) 394 237
Email: consumer.ccuk@coats.com
www.coatscrafts.co.uk

Fiskars UK Ltd
Newland Avenue
Brackla Industrial Estate,
Bridgend,
Glamorgan CF31 2XA
Tel: (01656) 655 595
www.fiskars.com
Craft products.

Franklin & Sons
13-15 St. Botolph's Street
Colchester
Essex CO2 7DU
Tel: (01206) 563 955
Sewing machines.

Fred Aldous
37 Lever Street
Manchester M1 1LW
Tel: (0161) 236 4224
Mail-order craft supplier.

John Lewis Partnership
Oxford Street
London W1A 1EX
Tel: (020) 7629 7711
www.johnlewis.com
Haberdashery. Check the website for a
full list of shops.

The Janome Centre
Southside
Breadbury, Stockport,
Cheshire SK6 2SP
Tel: (0161) 666 6011

Perivale Gutermann Ltd
Bullsbrook Road
Hayes, Middlesex UB4 0JR
Tel: (020) 8589 1600
Threads and zips.

MacCulloch and Wallis
25-26 Dering Street,
London W16 0BH
Tel: (020) 7629 0311
Email: macculloch@wallis.co.uk
www.macculloch-wallis.co.uk

Selectus
The Uplands, Biddulph,
Stoke on Trent ST8 7RH
Tel: (01782) 522 316
Email: sales@selectus.co.uk
www.selectus.co.uk

Stitches
355 Warwick Road
Olton
Solihull B91 1BQ
Tel: (0121) 706 1048
www.needle-craft.com
Embroidery and sewing materials.

Velcro
Unit 1
Aston Way
Middlewich,
Cheshire CU10 0HS
Tel: (01606) 738 806

Vilene Retail
Lowfield Business Park
Elland,
West Yorks MX5 9DX
Tel: (01422) 327 9000
Interfacing and fusible web.

NEW ZEALAND

**Embroidery and Patchwork
Supplies**
Private Bag 11199
600 Main Street
Palmerston North 5320
Tel: (06) 356 4793
Fax: (06) 355 4594
Toll Free in New Zealand 0800 909
600
Email: stitches@needlecraft.co.nz
www.needlecraft.co.nz

The Embroiderer
140 Hinemoa St
Birkenhead
Auckland
Tel: (09) 419 0900

Homeworks
First Floor Queens Arcade
Queen St
Auckland Central
Tel: (09) 366 6119

Nancy's Embroidery
273 Tinakori Rd
Thorndon
Wellington
Tel: (04) 473 404

Hands Ashford NZ Ltd
5 Normans Road
Elmwood
Christchurch
Tel/Fax: (03) 355 9099
Email: hands.craft@clear.net.nz

Spotlight Stores
Whangarei (09) 430 7220
Wairau Park (09) 444 0220
Henderson (09) 836 0888
Panmure (09) 527 0915
Manukau City (09) 263 6760
Hamilton (07) 839 1793
Rotorua (07) 343 6901

New Plymouth (06) 757 3575
Gisborne (06) 863 0037
Hastings (06) 878 5223
Palmerston North (06) 357 6833
Porirua (04) 238 4055
Wellington (04) 472 5600
Christchurch (03) 377 6121
Dunedin (03) 477 1478
www.spotlight.net.nz

AUSTRALIA
Lincraft Stores
Adelaide:
Shop 3.01, Myer Centre
Rundle Mall
Adelaide, SA 5000
Tel: (08) 8231 6611
Brisbane:
Shop 237, Myer Centre
Queen Street
Tel: (07) 3221 0064
Canberra:
Shop DO2/DO3, Canberra Centre
Bunda Street
ACT 2601
Tel: (02) 6257 4516
Melbourne:
Australia on Collins
Shop 320, 303 Lt. Collins Street
Melbourne VIC 3000
Tel: (03) 9650 1609
Perth:
St. Martins Arcade
Hay Street
Perth WA 6000
Tel: (08) 9325 1211
Sydney:
Gallery Level, Imperial Arcade
Pitt Street
Sydney NSW 2000
Tel: (02) 9221 5111

Spotlight Stores
Branches throughout Australia
VIC (03) 9684 7477
TAS (03) 6234 6633
NSW (02) 9899 3611
QLD (07) 3878 5199
SA (08) 8410 8811
WA (08) 9374 0966
NT (08) 8948 2008

SOUTH AFRICA

Free State Embroidery
64 Harley Road
Oranjesig,
Bloemfontein 9301
Tel: (051) 448 3872

Durbanville Needlecrafters
No. 1 44 Oxford
Oxford Street
Durbanville,
Cape Town 7550
Tel: (021) 975 7361

Groote Kerk Arcade
39 Adderly Street
Cape Town 8000
Tel: (021) 461 6941

Crafty Supplies
Stadium on Main
Main Road
Claremont 7700
Tel: (021) 671 0286

Stitch 'n' Stuff
140 Lansdowne Road
Claremont,
Durban 7700
Tel: (021) 674 4059

Nimble Fingers
Shop 222
Kloof Village Mall
Village Road
Kloof 3610
Tel: (031) 764 6283

Simply Stitches
2 Topaz Street
Albenarle
Germiston
Johannesburg 1401
Tel: (011) 902 6997

Golden Stitches
14 Thrush Avenue
Strelitzia Garden Village
Randpark Ridge Ext 47
Johannesburg 2156
Tel/Fax: (011) 795 3281

Pied Piper
69 1st Avenue
Newton Park
Port Elizabeth 6001
Tel: (041) 365 1616

Habby Hyper
284 Ben Viljoen Street
Pretoria North
0182
Tel: (012) 546 3568

Index